A Game Warden's Adventure

Humorous Short Stories of a
Career North Carolina Wildlife Officer

CONLEY MANGUM

North Carolina Wildlife Enforcement Sergeant
October 1, 1979 – December 1, 2007

Copyright 2016, Conley Mangum.

All rights reserved. No parts of this book may be reproduced or transmitted in any form or by any means without the expressed written permission of the author. Requests for permission should be addressed to hcmangum@suddenlink.net.

A Game Warden's Adventure:
Humorous Short Stories of a Career North Carolina Wildlife Officer
ISBN: 978-0-692-82421-4

Cover and interior design by Stephanie Whitlock Dicken.
Edited by Bethany Bradsher.

All rights reserved worldwide.

Preface

I started writing this book, mainly, just to relive some great times working a great career and to give my family a look at some of the adventures, both funny and dangerous, that I lived through. I loved being a Game Warden. Every day was different, most people looked up to you, and I remembered hearing countless comments from various men and women saying that they had always wanted to be a Game Warden. My response was always, "You won't become one if you don't try." I tried, and I did it. Some days I would get into my patrol vehicle and ask, "What do I want to do today? Do I want to dedicate the workday to duck hunting or deer hunting? Do I want to work bank fishing in a small Jon boat on the creeks or put the big boat on the water and work checking boating safety equipment on Kerr or Gaston Lakes?" As an officer, I loved that dilemma.

Later when I was promoted to Sergeant, that question didn't come up as often, but I still had a lot of time to do the things that I loved to do. My day as Sergeant was planned around what my officers in the field were doing, as I would normally assist them if I wasn't in a meeting. While working with my officers I was usually dropped out in a field to remotely work the mechanical deer or to watch hunters in the area. Sometimes I was dropped off on the bank of the Roanoke River to monitor a certain section for over-the-limit striper fishing. If any violations were detected, I would call the officer whom I was working with and give them the location, description of the vehicle or boat and the nature of the violation. That officer would then make the stop and either issue a citation or make an arrest.

Working as a Wildlife Officer was fun and exciting work, and I wanted my children to read about some of the exciting and even dangerous things I did in that job. I wanted them to know that life is short and you have to have a career that you love. Because life is so short, a person has to be able to laugh at stupid things he does, and while most people will not share those laughable moments with others, I do share because I like to see other people smile, even if it's going to cost me a little kidding down the road. This is why I wanted to focus on some of the funnier sides of Wildlife Law Enforcement. I did not write this to belittle anyone or the position of a North Carolina State Wildlife Officer, but only to show that we all do some stupid things while in training and throughout our career. I've made a lot of friends during my career as a "Rabbit Sheriff", "Coon Constable" or even "Mr. Green Jeans" with people in the counties that I have work. Some of the people that I befriended did not know what a Wildlife Protector was or what they did.

They were amazed that the State of North Carolina had officers that would stop their boats on the lake to make sure the boater had all the proper safety equipment.

But the closest friends I made were the officers with whom I worked. During long cold nights, working night deer hunting (or "firelighting"), or boating, we had nothing to do but talk. The more you worked with an officer, the more personal your conversations usually became, usually about family life. We were therapy for each other, and sometimes we could offer good advice to our buddies or laugh with them. If that didn't happen we could always share where we got half off pizza or buffets. Both were good.

There have been a lot of books written about game wardens, and except for different climates and wildlife, the enforcement duties and detail planning were essentially the same. The early morning and late evening work details, both on very cold trapping, deer or duck hunting details or very hot, mosquito and snake-infested duties, were all planned the same way — hurry to get to your assigned location without being seen, throw the parachute over the patrol vehicle or hunker down in marsh grass, wait and try not to swat mosquitoes as to give your location away. But how did we know where to work? Certainly, we knew when the stripers were running in the Roanoke River near Weldon, NC, and we knew there would be a lot of boat traffic there. Prior to dove or duck seasons we would check for high populations of birds in one area and then walk in or fly over to check for bait bringing the birds in.

The real help, however, came from sportsmen who had heard about bait being placed in a particular area or one of their hunting members constantly killing monster bucks, multiple times during a season, but never cleaning the deer at the club. Or maybe we would get leads from dove hunters in a field watching and hearing particular hunters doing a lot of shooting and seeing them throwing their doves in the woods only to pick them up after we had left a field. Sometimes the report was from a known violator or poacher telling on a rival violator. When turkey were being stocked in Warren County, my first duty station, some of the poachers of deer or stripers became very protective of them and would let me know when and where turkey were seen and how many. This information helped our Wildlife Biologist, and the officer, keep up with the populations. They would give me reports of trucks riding by a field early in the morning or late in the afternoon trying to shoot a turkey from the vehicle. There are hundreds of examples of illegal activities that a Game Warden would never know about if it were not for the sporting public. So to those people I say thank you for caring and thank you, that with your help, yours and my grandsons and granddaughters can hunt, fish and boat and enjoy what I and others like me worked so hard to protect for almost 30 years — some to the point of giving their lives for this calling.

Most importantly, I lovingly and apologetically dedicate this book to my wife, Margaret, of, now, 38 years and my children Kristen Porter and Jenna Hardee.

Me and my beautiful partner in life, Margaret

Unknowingly, I put all three of the people that I love the most through some terrible times. I loved my job, but it took me away from them on holidays with the family, camping or cookouts, and sometimes school events that I should have attended. I caused Margaret to have a lot of sleepless nights alone at home when I would be out all night and unable to call home to assure her everything was OK, because of my location or lack of a phone. It was Margaret who looked after our children when they were sick and I had to work. I remember when Kristen and Jenna had gotten a little older and one of them asked me, "Why can't we go camping or to cookouts like other families do?" It broke my heart to hear that, but it was true. I did try to do better to keep our family close and do some things with them, but most of that job fell to Margaret. She was the glue for our family. She was the one who worked a full-time job and carried our children to child care just to be able to buy groceries and nothing else, while I was out having fun. I'm sorry for being so selfish, and thank you.

In The Beginning

It was November of 1978 when I applied to become a Wildlife Officer. I was working with Westinghouse Elevators and was living on Harbor Island, just across the Intercostal Waterway going to Wrightsville Beach, North Carolina. I had been doing elevator work for about seven years and had decided that I needed to do something that was a little less dangerous. One day I was reading the newspaper at the kitchen table and looking in the help wanted ads. I noticed an ad seeking applicants to be Wildlife Enforcement Officers. I wasn't sure what they did for a living, but it sounded good to me. All that I knew was that I had been working in elevator shafts, some days not even seeing the sun, and I needed to be outside. I drove to the Employment Security Commission in Wilmington, North Carolina, asked for an application, took it home to fill it out and returned it the next day. I was given a date to return and on that date, I was there bright and early.

I remember taking some type of written test and then a finger dexterity test. All I had to do was pick up a peg about a half inch long, place it into a small washer and then insert the peg into a hole and to keep this up for a certain amount of time, seeing how many I could get into the hole. It was hard for me to believe that all I had to do was to put a peg into a hole and then I would be given a job carrying a gun, driving a high speed pursuit vehicle, operating a boat at night and catching wildlife violators. All of this, and getting a paycheck too! Well, it wasn't quite that simple. The application process lasted about five months, from January until May. I had physicals, was fingerprinted, and had background checks done on me and interviewed before a board.

While I was in Chapel Hill, waiting for my turn to be interviewed, Major Ray Johnson, who was in charge of the wildlife officer srcrui school, called me out of the waiting room and told me he wanted me to see a doctor concerning the ring finger on my left hand. While in my junior year at Northern High School in Durham playing in a football game against Garner High School, I had injured my left hand ring finger during a play. I played defensive middle guard, or "nose" guard, right in front of the center. The center snapped the ball to the quarterback and I lunged forward. When we met helmet to helmet, I pushed the offensive center to my right and reached for the fullback with my left hand just as the bull, I mean fullback, charged up the middle. All I could get on him was my left ring finger and that got caught in his belt loop. It's not the best way to make a tackle, and the end result was that I tore ligaments in that finger, causing me not to be able to bend it.

I had two surgeries on that hand, and to this day I cannot bend that finger.

When the doctor walked into the room I really didn't know what to expect. He was a small-framed guy, as I remember, with glasses, and he walked up to me and told me to cross my arms, right over left at the wrist and to grasp his hands. He then told me that he was going to try to get loose and he wanted me to try to hold him and keep him from getting loose. Noticing right away that his hands were small and really soft, remembering that I had been doing heavy steel construction for about 8 years and not wanting this test to knock me out of the wildlife school after having passed the peg-in-the-hole test, I clamped down REALLY hard. He began to holler, "Wait a minute, wait a minute, wait a minute!" Well, not wanting to disfigure the very man I was trying to impress, I eased up just a little. The doctor then began trying to get loose from my grip, but he couldn't. He then told Major Johnson that there was nothing wrong with me, and I headed back out to the interview waiting room to wait for my turn.

We had to wait a couple of weeks for our results but when they came, I had made it to the North Carolina Wildlife Enforcement Officer Recruit School located at the Institute of Government in Chapel Hill, NC. Now getting in the first school was one thing, but there were two schools that you had to attend to become a Wildlife Enforcement Officer. The first school lasted three weeks and what they taught us there was, if you want this job you will not quit. And the training consisted of anything that they could do to you to make you quit. This included tearing up your room while you were on the PT field at 0530 in the morning, a LOT of running, tumbling relay races, running the bleachers and any other activity the instructor could think of. We hated this guy because of how much he loved his job.

I usually lucked out on the room "rearrangement" event because my room was at the end of the hall and I think they ran out of dirt before they got to my room. Either that or they really, really liked and respected me —-nah. It definitely was not that. Usually my bed and closets were torn up but other guys had dirt thrown in the rooms. Everything had to be cleaned up before class at 0800. There was mental stress that included being yelled at, classroom instruction from 0800 to 1600, and a test given every day on some subject they were teaching. This usually included the game and fish laws that contained hundreds of pages of laws and regulations, 90 percent of which I had never heard of before. This required that you study at night from 1900 until 2100 after another PT in the afternoon, and then lights out at 2100. You were physically and mentally exhausted at the end of the day.

The classrooms were fairly small and got a little warm because of the officers' body heat from PT that morning. Of course that made it harder to stay awake while listening to the instructor talk. Our main Game Law instructor was actually a professor at UNC-Chapel Hill. Now this guy was brilliant. I believe he actually wrote the Fish and Game law for the state of North Carolina.

His manner and very soft monotone voice, though, were not conducive to staying awake in a warm classroom of exhausted officers. On top of this, he drank tea. Not just the traditional southern sweet ice tea, oh no. He put hot water in a coffee cup after every break and when he returned to class, he would dip his tea bag into the cup. Up and down, up and down, it seemed like he dipped his tea bag in his special tea cup every ten seconds for eight hours a day — very methodical, not too fast and not too slow. All of the officers in the room struggled to keep from going to sleep, sometimes even spitting into their hand and wiping their eyes with it.

One officer sat directly in front of the instructor's desk, and I mean dead center – the front seat, three feet from the instructor. One day I was watching the officer with his head bent over in his left hand and his elbow on the table, looking intently at his Wildlife Protector book. I was thinking, "Now here is a guy who has this school figured out. Not only is he on top of his game with PT, but he finds the energy to follow along in his book and learn the game laws. This guy is going to make a great officer one day." That is, until his head slipped from his left hand and hit the table and the officer fell out in the floor, with all of his books scattered on the floor. Our professor stopped dipping his tea bag, looked over the desk at the officer on the floor and without showing any expression on his face leaned back and began dipping that damn tea bag and talking again, very softly and very monotone. That made everyone in the classroom bust out laughing and gave us enough energy to stay awake until the next break. It also gave us something else to do during class and that was to watch Walter very closely to see if he would fall out again. He did come very close many times but then so did the rest of us. We just weren't the first to go down. As tired as you were, though, you hated to go to bed at night, because that just meant the next day was coming sooner.

We were up at 0500 and on the field at 0530 for PT, which consisted of a lot of running around the track and counting the steps and seats of the bleachers around the track field, while running up and down them. You were then asked how many steps there were, and if everyone did not have the same number, you ran them again. Each time we ran the bleachers, our instructor would change your running pattern so that the number of steps always changed. We also did a lot of tumbling relay races against each other. The losers of this race had to tumble down the course again while the winners just watched. I HATED this part of the school. I would always get really dizzy and REALLY sick. I was so dizzy that I couldn't find my line to run back to. I would then stay sick until the next day.

After the first week was over, someone mentioned taking motion sickness pills, and so I bought some over the weekend. They kept me from getting sick while going through the tumbling relay races, but they also made me sleepy for the rest of the day. When we had finished PT, about 0630 if we hadn't screwed up, we went to breakfast and then had to be in class at 0800. We had class until 1600 and then had to be dressed in workout clothes and out on the track at 1630 for PT. The afternoon PT was sometimes substituted with a softball game against some of the UNC Intramurals teams. After that, it was showers, supper and then back in class from 1900 until 2100. This time period was usually a study hall period designed to help you remember something from class that day, or remember anything for that matter. I weighed about 195 pounds when I went into the three-week school, and came out at 187 pounds.

We also ran a lot of 50-yard suicide drills, and of course that was made into a game for the instructors as well. That meant we would line up into two groups, one behind the other. On the whistle the first officer would run to the 10-yard line and back to the starting line, then run to the 20-yard line and back to the starting line, run to the 30-yard line and back to the starting line, and finally run to the 50-yard line and back to the starting line, touching the hand of the next man in line. Then it was his turn for the same drill with the officer that just finished going to the back of the line. When the first man to run made it back to the first position in line, the round was over. Whichever line finished first got to watch the losing line of officers run the drill again. I hated this drill.

Next we would head to the track in the same lines used for the previous drill and start running side by side, with the shortest man in each line leading his line around the track. I always led one group and Danny Pierce led the other group, because we had 29-inch legs. Everyone else had normal legs. The tallest man was always in the back griping and complaining about how slow we were leading the group. But what could they expect? My legs had to run twice as far as their legs to go the same distance. I did what I could as far as my running speed was concerned, but it was never enough. After the first mile and a half, I would cut everyone loose to run their own pace for the last couple of miles. That way the real runners in the school got a chance to shine for the instructors, and Danny and I got to fight for the next-to-last place trophy. It seemed that the first three-week school was designed to see if you wanted the job. Instructors, especially PT instructors, did what they could to get us to quit the school. We did anything we could do to stay. The biggest thing that we could do was to not say, "I quit."

The afternoon Physical Training session was tiring but different, and it was actually a lot of fun. The eighteen of us got to play the college students at the University of North Carolina at intramural sports and we played a LOT of softball. We held our own with these younger guys, although we didn't win every game we played, sometimes because we couldn't finish them. Some games had to be called because some young student was running his mouth off to us: "Hey old man, where's the cane?" "You'll need thicker glasses if you're going to catch that high ball!" "Next time take some Geritol!." These were just some of the MANY comments we heard. Sometimes this hurt our feelings. Sometimes it led us to "accidentally" run into a student when we should have been sliding into a base or maybe tagging a student a little too hard after we pushed him off the base, "accidentally" of course. Why, I even saw a couple of "accidents" happen when a student was running to third and the shortstop on our team stepped into the base line. This sometimes caused terrible and violent collisions. What could you expect? We were older and more uncoordinated than these young guys AND we were mentally exhausted after a hard day of class. Now that I think about it, it really wasn't our fault at all. It was the Wildlife Commission's fault for getting us so tired and making us more ill and uncoordinated.

North Carolina Wildlife Recruit School
Chapel Hill, North Carolina, 1979

This first Wildlife Recruit School lasted three weeks, and then you were hired according to how you placed in the school. There were eight hundred applicants the year I applied with twenty applicants selected for the school. Two of these left for personal reasons, and I finished fifth overall in the school. If you got through the three-week school, you were assigned to a training officer in either a part-time or a permanent position, and the following summer you were invited back to an eleven-week school.

After the three-week school ended in August, I was hired on October 1, 1979. I worked some with a training officer, but after about a month or two I was on my own. My Sergeant, N.G. Crews, asked if I had a Wildlife Protector book and I said yes. He then said, "Go enforce the law but do not get into anything over your head. If you see something that may escalate or something you don't understand, call me and we can always go back to get them." With that advice in mind, I got in my patrol vehicle and set out to enforce the game laws. I hadn't driven too far, maybe four or five miles, when I saw some guys fishing. I glanced at my Wildlife Protector book, looked at the fishing laws and headed their way. When I pulled up, there were three guys fishing in the pond. I walked up to them and asked if they had any luck and proceeded to ask them for their fishing licenses. Two of the men produced a fishing license and the other asked, "Do you need a fishing license to fish in a private pond?" I stated, "Yes, sir". He said that he didn't have one but said that he would go get one if he had to. Me being the kindhearted, newly sworn Game Warden that I was AND considering I hadn't been given a ticket book yet, AND that I had not been told how to write a ticket yet, I decided to let him go purchase the fishing license but warned him, "Don't let it happen again!"

About ten years later I was in a 7-Eleven store in Warrenton, NC and a man approached me and asked if a person needed a fishing license to fish in a private pond. I said "No, not if the body of water lies entirely on one man's land. Why?" He said, "About 10 years ago a game warden checked me and told me he needed a fishing license to fish in a farm pond." "Probably a rookie," I said.

In May of 1980 all officers in the 1979 school returned to the Institute of Government in Chapel Hill for eleven weeks of more fun and relaxation. And really the eleven-week school, though long, was not too bad. The instructors treated you like you were almost equals, but just almost. We were taught the subjects we needed to be effective officers in the field in more depth. The training consisted of game and fish laws, all of the courses now taught in the Basic Law Enforcement Training schools to be certified as a law enforcement officer, courtroom testimony, firearms training, how to set and locate traps set in creeks, and boating enforcement, which consisted of the classroom portion of boating rules of the road and boating laws. We then went to Lake Wheeler in Raleigh, NC to learn about boat operation.

Many of the officers who attended the Wildlife Recruit School had never, for whatever reason, been in a boat, much less operated a boat at night while chasing another boat maneuvering to get away from them. Most of these officers were from the mountains and really just didn't get around large bodies of water.

There was also Pursuit Driving, Explosives, Handcuffing Techniques and exposure to different drugs, including one State Bureau of Investigation (SBI) instructor who lit some marijuana in a bowl and passed it around the SMALL room for us to smell. It was strange to me that it took about thirty minutes for that bowl to get around the room with eighteen guys sitting in two rows, two men to a table. Good thing it was right before lunch. We learned how to disarm an assailant in worst case scenarios, (like multiple suspects wrestling one officer), how to direct traffic, strategies for riot control complete with tear gas, how to set up and work night hunting details and many, many more topics.

Then there was the boxing. What was dreaded most in the Recruit School was Defensive Tactics, which was taught in about the eighth and ninth weeks of training. It was held off until the eighth week of school so that each officer who made it that far would be in shape to endure the defensive fighting without getting severely hurt. I remember we held the boxing training on the right side of the dorm at the Institute of Government in Chapel Hill, NC, near some trees, I guess so the public could not see us flailing on each other. All of the recruits would form a circle, and two fighters would get into the ring.

My friend Danny and I were matched up first, I guess because of our short legs. There was no holding back. If you did hold back, you got additional time in the ring. We started out with me hitting Danny in the head while he covered up for a couple of minutes, then he got to hit me in the head as I covered up. This was just the warm up, and next we fought for two minutes. Neither one of us were great boxers, and I remember there was a time when we were both jabbing lefts at the same time and both connecting at the same time, with both of our heads flying backward at each jab. Then we would both throw a right and both connect AGAIN at the same time. This sucked. At one point we actually acted like we knew what we were doing, and the next thing I knew, Danny threw a right and hit me in the left forehead. The whole left side of my body went numb as if I had been hit in my funny bone, the whole length of my body. It didn't hurt too bad, but I just couldn't swing my left fist back at him for a while. If I had just had feeling back in that left arm, he would have paid dearly. I still had my right fist, though. We were both glad when it was over.

Warrenton, NC
SEPTEMBER 1979

Approximately one month after the eleven-week Wildlife Basic Training School I received a call from the Colonel of Wildlife Resources. The first thing he asked was, "Are you ready to go to work?" I said, "Yes, sir." He said, "Good. Your duty station will be a temporary assignment and will be in Swan Quarter, NC. Go find somewhere to live and be ready to work the morning of October 1." I said, "Yes sir, thank you." I turned to Margaret and told her that I had a duty station close to Nags Head, NC. I didn't have the heart to tell her it was Swan Quarter, NC. Swan Quarter, NC, in 1979, was a very small town with an abundance of fishing, hunting, crabbing and about anything else you wanted to do in the wild. It was a single game warden's paradise, but it was the exact opposite of Wrightsville Beach, NC, where we were living when I applied with Wildlife Resources. I built it up for her as best I could, but I knew it was going to be tough for her. There were no nice restaurants, movie theaters or malls. While a wonderful place for those that call the mosquito the state bird and love seclusion, my wife would have a hard time. We had discussed this living situation before I was offered my duty station, though, and she gave me her blessing.

Approximately one week later, I received another call from the Colonel and I was told my duty assignment had been changed from Swan Quarter, NC to Warrenton, NC, and I still needed to find a house and report, ready to work, in two weeks. So I promptly pulled out the North Carolina state map and tried to locate Warrenton, NC. When I did find it, I really liked the location, especially as a newly married couple and especially compared to Swan Quarter, NC. Warrenton is located about twenty miles east of Interstate I-85, approximately ten miles from the North Carolina/Virginia state line. It was between Kerr Lake, an 800-mile shoreline freshwater lake and Lake Gaston, a 300-mile shoreline freshwater lake. Some of both of these lakes were in Warren County, and I would be spending A LOT of time patrolling these lakes. Kerr Lake would be a paradise to work, as it had multiple state parks for camping and water skiing, and both lakes had excellent striper fishing. This would be a much better fit for us to start a new life together. Little did I know how hard it would be for my wife, Margaret — being in a new place, not knowing anyone, not having a job and having me away at work day and night at a job that I loved. Sometimes she and I still talk of those times and how hard and lonely they were for her, even thirty-eight years later. I certainly did pick a good, understanding and patient lady to be my wife.

Margaret and I were living in Warren County, North Carolina, at 101 Reid Circle when I started my job, and our rent was only $125 a month, versus $300 for our apartment on Harbor Island at Wrightsville Beach, NC. We had come to Warrenton approximately two weeks earlier to look for a place to stay. We didn't find anything in the newspaper or by asking around, so we left Warrenton and returned to Durham, where we were staying with my mother in the house that I grew up in. We were about twenty miles out of Warrenton, and we decided to go back and try again to try and find a house to rent. We walked into Selby Benton's furniture store on Main Street in Warrenton, where I introduced myself to some of the guys standing around and told them that I was going to be the next game warden in the county. One of the guys standing there said that he knew of a place that was going to be available within the next couple of days, and he told us how to find Emily Thompson's house. We drove over there and it so happened that the Reid sisters and their husbands, including Emily, were sitting in the backyard of Emily's house at a picnic table eating watermelon. Margaret and I walked up, introduced ourselves and gladly joined in. We then asked them about the house and if it was available to rent. Emily said that she had a house that may be available, but we would talk about it after we ate watermelon.

During this time, we were asked a lot of questions about where we were from, how long we had been married, how many children we had, what brought us to Warrenton and at least another hour of questions.

We also had the honor of Emily telling us about her husband, Tim, who had served in World War II, and the Reid sisters' history in Warren County. I had never done anything like this, but I had seen it on the Andy Griffith Show a few times and I must admit, I really liked having to slow down for a while to just talk. All four of the sisters had deep Southern accents and were as sweet as a lady could be. We laughed a lot, and after the watermelon was gone Emily spoke up and said that the house was hers and it was available.

We walked to the house and went through the front door, which opened to a living room with a fireplace to the right and separate dining room to the left. Through the dining room was the kitchen with washer and dryer hookups. If, after coming through the front door, you walked straight, you walked into a short hallway running right and left. In the middle of the hall was a floor oil furnace. During our first years in Warrenton there was a national oil shortage. The only way a person new to the county could get fuel oil was if an established resident of the county with good credit not only recommended you, but also signed for your deposit with the oil company. Emily and her husband Tim gladly did that for us. There was only one bathroom in the house, and for the time being that was enough. There was no air conditioning in the home, but we knew we could work with that if the price was right. There was a fireplace in the living room that would come in handy.

After touring the house, I asked Emily what she was asking for rent and she said that they had just had some work done to the house, including painting it, and she would just have to get $125 a month. I looked at Margaret and tried not to smile. I said that it would be hard, but I thought we could pay that much. We were really excited and before you knew it, we had a home. About a year later, I bought a Craft wood stove insert for the fireplace. I then bought a chainsaw. Large landowners around the county would let me cut wood for the fireplace, and for several years, until we moved, we heated the whole house with wood. It was kind of messy with dust and dirt, but that wood heat sure felt good when I got in from a firelighting detail at 0200 when it was 25 degrees outside. Loggers I knew that hunted regularly would also bring me a load of white and red oak and hickory in a ten-wheel pulp wood truck. These logs were about six-feet long and yielded about four to five cords of eighteen-inch logs for the wood stove. The price was about $100.

First Day of Work

When I first came to the Commission on October 1, 1979 I didn't know a lot about hunting. My dad took my three brothers and me hunting as much as he could to Camp Butner, NC for deer or to Stem, NC for dove and small game hunting. But what I learned, I really learned on my own. We always hunted on Thanksgiving Day when I was growing up, leaving home early in the morning and coming back to eat the Thanksgiving feast that Mom had spent all morning cooking for us. Whenever I wanted to hunt by myself, I would get my wagon and walk along some of the more heavily traveled roads near my house in Durham, NC to pick up drink bottles. I got two cents a piece for a bottle. I'd save up about 75 cents and then go to Riley's Store on the corner of Guess Road and Carver Street in Durham and buy a box of twenty-two bullets. No signature or ID to produce, not even calling my parents for permission – just 75 cents from a nine-year-old boy so he could go hunting. And man, did I love being in the woods. I hunted or shot all day long on Saturdays and was home before the streetlight came on. I tracked animals that I didn't know existed. I would climb about thirty feet, halfway up a rocky ledge next to the Eno River and a five-mile walk from home, and I'd sit on that ledge most of the day and just look and listen. There was so much to see from that vantage point, especially when the leaves were off the trees and a warm sun was beaming down. Gun control back then was just proper sight alignment and sight picture on anything worthy of shooting, especially sticks floating down the river.

Lieutenant James Duke, Captain Rueben Crumpton and Sergeant N.G. Crews came by to get me at the house on 101 Reid Circle that first day, but before I could go to work, I first had to put my badge on. Margaret did the honors for me in the dining room, and I was now ready for my first day on the job. Dove season was in, and so what did we do? We drove to the Country Kitchen on Norlina Road and started drinking coffee. Here I was ready to go out and "law" someone, and we were drinking coffee. I must have drunk a pot before we left to find some dove hunters. It turned out to be an uneventful day, but it was fun. The hardest part was trying figure out how 100 different shotguns were loaded and unloaded, so I could check them for a plug. Half of the time I got the owner to extract all of the shells from the magazine and then reload the gun so I could count the shells going in.

There was a law at that time stating that shotguns had to be plugged and incapable of holding more than three shells. That meant two shells in the magazine and one shell in the chamber. It applied to all game when I first began working, but today the law has been relaxed quite a bit and that prohibition only applies to migratory birds, dove, and duck. One thing I did learn while checking guns was that if you don't know how a certain gun works, you should let the hunter place the shells in the shotgun magazine himself but watch him closely. I learned to always attempt to put the third shell in the magazine myself. This training period didn't last long, because when you checked that many shotguns you would get blisters on your thumb. But man, what a great day. I couldn't believe I actually got paid to do this type of work. On my second day I would be working with an officer from Franklin County named Burley Clark.

Burley Clark

Burley Clark, a veteran Wildlife Officer stationed in Franklin County, NC, was one of my training officers about one day a week. Our work area, Area 4 District 3, consisted of Warren, Franklin and Vance Counties in northern NC along the I-85 Interstate. One day, Burley and I were working hunting in the lower part of Warren County near Shocco Gun Club in the southern part of the county and we were near the end of Christmas Road, a dead end dirt road. I was driving, and at this point I had to turn into an abandoned house's dirt driveway to turn the patrol vehicle around. I started back up the road when I saw about six to eight baby turkeys, called "poults", running across the road. I got a good feeling just thinking that I would be protecting wildlife like these from poachers. I stopped the patrol vehicle in the middle of the dirt road and asked Burley, "Are they baby turkeys?" Being the professional that he was, he took his pipe out of his mouth and just said, "Boy, those aren't baby turkeys, they're guineas." I think I really impressed him that day with my knowledge of wildlife. Yes sirree, my wildlife career was off to a good start. This was also about the time I learned to keep my mouth shut unless spoken to.

Burley loved to smoke his pipe. I think he kept it going the whole time he worked. The only time that I can't remember it going was when he was going to reload it. He would open the door and bang it on the side of the car at the bottom of the door about four or five times. If you were trying to get some sleep that would surely wake you up. He would then open his tobacco pouch and drag his pipe from right to left. He'd look at it and if it weren't just right, he would top it off. Then he would pack the tobacco down just right with his thumb. After it was reloaded, he would pull out his lighter. This lighter was turned to the highest setting. He would place the lighter over the tobacco, light it and would puff hard and fast about five or six times. When the smoke started to roll, she was ready for another hour. I never saw a pipe last as long as his. It must have been because tobacco cost was high and he was so tight with his money.

Using an aircraft to find hunters, both legal and illegal, was a tremendous help for catching poachers. One thing the observer had to know were his county roads, and he needed to know them well enough that he could tell a patrol car where and when to pull into a certain "hole" in order to hide the vehicle from a poacher passing by. Since Burley Clarke had been working longer than Julian Alman and I, Burley was usually the observer. The aircraft that was in service when I first reported to work was a Super J, front and back two seater. The passenger, sitting in the back, had a stick to control the plane's movement up and down and in turns. The pilot controlled everything else. While in flight, the pilot would usually give the observer control of the plane. The observer was normally the local officer in the county that we were working, and he knew his way around the county. This was the case unless the local officer got airsick like I did. I could fly at night, but make me an observer during daylight hours and I was a sick puppy. So having control of the plane in the rear seat was a good thing. One could fly to all the areas where reports of illegal hunting were occurring.

Once an activity was spotted on the ground, the controls were given back to the pilot, and the observer would then focus all of his attention to the boat or truck on the ground and call in its location to patrol vehicles stationed on the ground. Two or three patrol vehicles were usually stationed about four to five miles apart from each other. The observer, knowing the location of the "ground units," would then call in the nearest unit and direct him to the suspicious vehicle. Even on dark nights, the observer could see a light outline of the roads below and direct a ground unit through the various turns to make contact. There were some very large tracts of paper company land in my work area, and looking down from the aircraft, the area looked like a big black hole. This also was a big plus when working with an aircraft in those areas because any light source at all, even lighting a cigarette, could be seen by the aircraft observer. One tool that was highly prized by the observer was night vision equipment. This equipment amplified the ambient light in the area and would let the observer actually see the vehicle being watched. The instructions from the observer would let the ground unit know how far they were from the suspect's vehicle, what direction the suspect was headed, and whether he had stopped. If he had stopped, we would stop the ground unit and have him step out of the vehicle to listen for shots, or let them know if the suspect's vehicle had turned around and was headed back to the ground unit. In this case the observer would have the ground unit find a hiding spot until the suspects came by him. Burley was very good at working the ground units.

Another time, early on in my Wildlife career, I was stationed in Area 4, which was made up of Franklin, Vance and Warren Counties. Our area had the aircraft for a small game flight. These types of details were usually after the deer season, which went out between January 1 and the ending of the small game season on February 28, and also on holiday weekends when relatives of local farmers would come in to visit from other states. Most of these folks never had a hunting license. We began flying east of Louisburg, and our aircraft observer found some rabbit hunters in a large field with a big, thick grassy area in the middle of the field. Burley was the observer in the plane, and he called for me and Julian to check the hunters. We got to the field and Julian went to one side of the brush pile while I went to the other. I checked my men and was just standing there talking, when Burley called down to me and said, "You need to quit talking and start checking. We have other places to go." I remembered from that time on not to take a lot of time checking hunters while working with Burley on the AC.

One day, Burley and I were working deer hunting in Franklin County. After checking a couple of deer hunts, we got back into the patrol vehicle. Burley puffed on his pipe a couple times, turned and looked at me and told me that I would probably never make it with the Wildlife Commission because I was too nice of a guy. He told me that if I was thinking about leaving the WRC for any reason, I needed to go ahead and do it before I reached my five-year employment mark. "After that," he said, "you'll be too sorry to do any real work in the real world." If I had only known then what I know now!

In the old days, ground units had switches on the patrol vehicle – one to turn off the brake lights and backup lights and another to turn off the parking lights. With the parking lights off, a ground unit could actually follow the suspect vehicle anywhere from fifty to one hundred yards in a "blackout" and never be seen. We were trained to follow the suspect's taillights or even look about forty-five degrees out of our driver's window at the side of the road. As you look out of the driver side window, the road in front of you would actually get brighter and you could drive with your peripheral vision, because the night vision portion of your eyes are located around your pupils. You can do this because the rods in your eyes are located outside of the macula or center of the eye and it's the rods that are responsible for night vision or low light, but they are not able to pick up color. It was also important that you not let your patrol vehicle get too close to the suspect's vehicle while following him, because if the suspect applied his brakes, or used a Q-beam spotlight out of his window, the light would reflect off of the chrome of the patrol vehicle and give your position away. Where I lived in Warren County, I could leave the house at night to patrol firelighting by myself, work three to four hours and never turn on my headlights to drive.

One night while working firelighting with Burley in Franklin County near the Vance County line, we saw a small vehicle on another road parallel to our dirt road, and someone was shining a spotlight out of the passenger's window. Burley stopped our car and pulled in next to some trees near the road and let the shining vehicle continue down the road. Burley turned off the patrol vehicle headlights and caught up with the vehicle shining, which was a yellow Jeep CJ 5. Burley pulled in close enough to the truck to get his license plate and then turned on his blue lights. The truck slowed and pulled next to the ditch on the right but continued to move slowly down the road. This meant the passenger was looking for a place to throw a gun out of the truck. Burley hit the siren a couple of times, and the Jeep finally came to a stop beside a soybean field.

We both got out of our patrol vehicle and approached the Jeep on both sides of it, me on the passenger side and Burley on the driver's side. Suddenly the door opened on my side, and I saw the barrel of a rifle. I began yelling to throw the gun down, but the man continued to exit. I pulled my Smith and Wesson Model 19 357 magnum as the man made a complete exit and turned to look at me with his rifle at a port-of-arms carry position. Aiming my revolver at the center of his chest, I again yelled for the man to throw the gun down and he lobbed the gun into the soybean field on top of a plant. I had the man move to the other side of the truck where Burley was and I retrieved his rifle, a Remington Model 700 30-06 bolt action. I walked around to the left side of our patrol car and asked the man if he knew what he was doing by not obeying me. He told me that his wife had just bought him that gun and he didn't want to scratch it by throwing it in the ditch. I told him had he not put the gun down, he might not be using it again, ever. That was close, but Burley didn't know any of this was going on. He was talking to the driver of the Jeep because he knew him. Ole Burley passed away not too long ago, and a lot of wisdom left with him.

A GAME WARDEN'S ADVENTURE

Aircraft Details

One particular night, when I was stationed in Warren County, my patrol area had an aircraft detail in Halifax County. The area that I was assigned was Area 2, District 3, which consisted of Warren, Halifax and Northampton Counties. The area we would be working was just outside of Scotland Neck, NC, and Jim Ward would be our observer. Our detail would start at 2200 and we would usually work about four hours, longer if we had a lot of activity. By start, I mean all ground units would be in their assigned locations at 2200. We met at our Sergeant's house and he gave us our Signal 1, which was our "assigned location." My setup was not too far from Scotland Neck and was behind a barn next to the road. The aircraft took off and began circling our area to work, about 20 square miles, to find each officer's exact location.

Lying on the hood of the car and looking into the sky was a relaxing time for me, especially when the sky was clear. It was a cool night and I had my sleeping bag pulled over me to keep me warm. The sleeping bag and the warmth from the car hood from a recently driven car felt great. Because of that, we had to turn up our portable radios a little more than normal to wake us up in case we drifted off to sleep. On a clear night you could see forever, and as we lay there we would look for the aircraft. When we spotted it, we would then guide the aircraft to our location by using the "clock" method. The aircraft was always the clock and the nose of the plane always 1200. If we were to the left of the airplane's forward motion and the nose of the plane, we might say, "I am 1000 to you and about two miles". The pilot would adjust the aircraft left to his 1000 o'clock position and ask us to give him a light. I would then shine my flashlight straight into the air until the observer told us that he had our position. The aircraft would do this to all of the ground units.

Anyway, I had been working most of the day checking deer hunters along the Halifax and Warren County lines and did not have time to get supper before out aircraft detail began. I reached my Sig 1 about 2100 hours, pulled beside of a barn and threw my parachute over the vehicle. I sat in my setup for about an hour and was starving to death. Since there had been no activity, knowing that Scotland Neck was only a few miles away AND that Hardee's would be closing soon, I decided to leave my setup, drive to town blackout (no headlights) and get something to eat. I figured I could go and get something and be back at my setup before anyone noticed. The first thing I needed to know was where the aircraft was, so I walked to the edge of the road and listened for the airplane's engine. Nothing. I looked for aircraft lights moving in the sky. Again nothing. I walked back to the patrol vehicle and pulled out onto the road, blackout, and headed to town.

I was about a mile from my Sig 1 when the observer of the plane called me and said that he was watching a vehicle with no lights on, driving slowly down a road and that the vehicle was north of my Sig 1 about 2 miles. I had been spotted by my own aircraft! I made several turns trying to lose the plane but every time I turned, the observer would give the direction of the suspicious vehicle. I thought for a while and came up with a plan. I pulled the patrol vehicle over and called the observer. I asked if the vehicle he was watching was near a certain road and he called back that it was. I shined my flashlight up in the air and asked if he could see it. He said yes. I called back and told him that it was me, that I had heard a gunshot and was trying to locate it. By the directions he was giving me, I thought that he was guiding me to source of the shot. I turned on my headlights and told the observer that I was heading back to my Sig 1. I was STILL starving to death.

Not ever wanting to be caught starving again, I visited a friend of mine with the National Guard. I asked him for some MRE's (military Meals Ready to Eat) and he fixed me up. These MREs were not the newer MREs with the tan plastic outer layer now produced for our military but came in dark brown heavy plastic and contained dehydrated fruit and chocolate cookie and granola bars. I never went anywhere without my MREs. The best thing about them was that you could eat them cold or hot, if you had a heat source. One day while patrolling I decided that I was tired of eating cold beef stew. I realized that I was riding in a heat source. So I pulled my patrol car, which was a 1974 Plymouth Fury with a 440 engine and also the best four wheel drive to that date, over to the side of the road. I placed my beef stew on the engine manifold, closed the hood, and again, began my patrol. This being my first time doing this, I was unsure of the time needed to heat up my stew so I decided to give it thirty minutes. About twenty minutes into my cooking time, I began smelling beef stew, and at first it smelled really good. I pulled the car over, popped the hood open and saw my beef stew all over the engine and firewall. Of course the stew bag got too hot and exploded. I decided to cut my cooking time to 10 minutes. Some officers did not like the MREs, but I loved them. Of course you had to eat them sparingly, as they had lots of calories and sodium. I don't think I ever worked again without a case of MREs in the trunk of my vehicle or in the plastic box in my boat.

Being the observer in a plane was really a lot of fun for me, but only at night. The noise in the plane was very loud from the engine. Because of that, we always had to wear a headset with a mike on it to talk either to the pilot or to the ground units. There were two buttons for the observer to transmit on, located on the left hand side of the plane under my side window. One button was for the ground unit and the other for talking privately to the pilot. This particular night we were working a detail just north of the Tar River near Greenville, NC.

I was eating watermelon-flavored Jolly Ranchers and just enjoying the flight. From just east of Greenville and on a clear night you could lights from different towns on the horizon. I could see lights from as far away as Morehead, Nags Head and even Cape Hatteras, about eighty miles as the crow flies. Looking west, you could see lights from Goldsboro, Wilson, Rocky Mount and even Raleigh, NC.

It was a great night to fly except for one thing; I started getting a little gas in my stomach. I opened a small window in the back of the plane, about two inches round, and tried to sneak some gas out without getting caught by the pilot. Well, that didn't work. As soon as I cut one, the pilot pressed the button on his headset and asked, "Did you just pass gas?" I pressed my button and said "Yeah. That fart smelled like watermelon." The pilot started laughing and then I got a call from one of the ground units asking, "That fart smelled like what?" It was then that I realized that I had pressed, not the button to the pilot but the button to all of my ground units. Of course I had to hear about that little incident for about a year. The pilots that I flew with after that night would make me open a little round vent in the side window in the back seat of the Maul we were flying in just in case I decided to eat watermelon Jolly Ranchers.

Other flights placed the officer on the ground in some pretty thick brush over small pine trees. The officer on the ground could not see five feet in front of him. The pilot would tell us to put our blaze orange caps on, and then he could see us and tell us which way the hunters were in relation to us. Again, using the clock method, the pilot could tell us that the groups of hunters were 0200 to our position and about 100 yards away. The ground officer would turn to the approximately 0200 position from the way he was facing and run, as best as he could, through the brush toward the hunters. Sometimes it took a little while to get to them because the hunters were also moving, following their rabbit or bird dogs, but the pilot would put us just in front of the hunters every time. This was also very dangerous for the officer.

One rabbit hunt that a pilot put me on had me starting out behind the hunters and trying to catch up with them. But as most hunters know, rabbits will start off in one direction and then run a big circle back to the starting point. This little maneuver orchestrated by my little furry friend put me in between the prey and hunters. As I was trying to get closer, I heard one hunter yell, "There's the rabbit!" and then the rabbit ran within five feet of me. I got behind the biggest tree I could find, a four-inch diameter pine tree, and tried to make my 5-foot-10, 230-pound frame three-and-a-half inches wide. I heard the shotgun blast and watched number 6 shot spray across the pine needle floor about eight feet in front of my "tree". I shouted, "Game warden, I need to check your license," and the hunters, a little startled, walked into view. I think they were as surprised at me being there as I was at having gotten in that situation. "Man, you could have been shot", one said. "Nah," I reassured them. "I was behind a tree."

Patrol Time

There was an old store near the intersection of the Baltimore Road and Lickskillet Road in lower Warren County that was operated by an older man and his mother. He was about 50 to 55 years old in the early 1980s, and his mother must have been in her 70s at that time. From time to time I would stop in and get a drink and just sit around and talk, not about anything in particular, just about anything and everything that came up. This store must have been a hundred years old and had stuff hanging everywhere. There was a potbelly stove in the middle of the store, and in the winter that stove was the sole source of heat. There is nothing like a wood fire when it's cold and damp outside. I never remember it being cold inside. As I would drink my drink, my eyes would wander around the store and I was amazed at the things that I saw. Washtubs, feed bags, an old glass display case (the top glass was cracked where someone had leaned too hard on it) with all kinds of knick-knacks in it, boxes of lye on the shelves, you need it and I think he had it.

One day I noticed an open box of double dip chocolate covered peanuts behind the counter and asked the owner how much the peanuts were. He told me and I said that I would take a small bag. He pulled out a small brown paper bag, opened it up and reached in and got a big handful and put them in the bag for me. I think he charged me a $1 for them. I bought a Coke and had a great lunch. They were delicious. Double dipped. They became my staple every time I was working in that area and went by the store. One day I was at the home of a friend, Eddie Strickland, who became a very good friend and shooting partner. Eddie lived in a farmhouse across from the Lickskillet Game Lands. The game land got its name, I am told, during the Civil War. I believe a group of Confederate soldiers had gotten themselves surrounded by Union troops. Instead of the Union troops attacking, they just put a siege on them and waited them out. The food got so scarce that the troops would "lick their skillets" so as not to waste any food. They later surrendered to the Union troops.

Anyway, I told Eddie about the peanuts at the store and that I would be stopping by there and getting some on the way from his house. He asked me if I liked them and I told him they were a staple for me when I came that way. He started laughing and told me to watch the owner for a while before I bought any peanuts and just see if he did anything unusual. I was more than a little curious, so when I left Eddie's I headed for the store. I went in, got a drink out of the drink box and sat down in the ladder back chair that became my seat near the potbelly wood stove. We talked for a while and I watched him closely to see what, if anything, would happen. I didn't notice anything unusual for a while as I watched him behind the old counter so I asked him for a small bag of peanuts while he was back there. He said, "Why sure," then reached down and scratched his private parts and put the same hand into the peanut box. He came out with a handful of peanuts and put them in the small brown bag. Not wanting to act surprised, I acted as if everything was great, paid for the peanuts and headed out to the car to leave. About a mile from the store I poured my double dipped peanuts out the window and began to appreciate Tom and Lance products just a little more than I once had. I did love those peanuts, though.

Another time I was in the store eating Tom's cheese crackers when I saw a hunter come in. I asked him if he had any luck and he said no. He said that he was bow hunting just down the road and always stopped at this store for lunch when he was down from Tarboro. He asked me how to become a game warden, and I gave him the application process and told him how hard the school was. He told me that he had always wanted to be a game warden, and about two years later he did. His name was Wayne Rudd, and he was stationed in Edgecombe County. I always heard good things about Wayne from his fellow officers and the public that knew him.

While living and working in Warren County I met a lot of people who are still my friends today. Some of the people I met didn't have the best of reputations in the wildlife field, but we got along very well. I always treated everyone that I checked with respect, and that paid off. I still try to do that today.

Another store that I frequented when I was nearby was Harvey's Store in Arcola. Mr. Harvey lived in a brick house beside the store and anytime I needed a break, Harvey's was where I went. It was a small store and carried just the basics for the people living in that area. The basics, for me, was a bologna and cheese sandwich. When I was a new officer I would tell Mr. Harvey what I wanted and he would make it for me. After a while, he told me to just make my own. As I entered the store, I would head straight to the back left corner where the cold food was and get out a long log of bologna. I carried it over to the cutting board, which also happened to be where the hoop cheese was located. I cut a thick slice of bologna and lay on my loaf bread. I then lifted the plastic cheese cover and sliced a generous portion of sharp hoop cheese, placing the cheese on top of my bologna. Next came mayo and a lot of black pepper. I added to my sandwich a large Snickers and a can drink. Total cost, $1.25. Although this was a lunch break, anyone and everyone in the store talked hunting and I got a chance to share newly enacted wildlife laws or even try to explain why certain laws on the books now were needed. I knew I could never convince the local farmers the new laws were needed, but what I really wanted was information concerning illegal hunting or trapping. And sometimes this paid off for me.

One day I was in Hardees on Norlina Road in Warrenton, and it was only the second time I had ever been in there. I ordered a sausage biscuit and coffee and looked for a seat. As I sat down, I noticed three or four men sitting at a booth in the back. One of the men got up and approached my table. He introduced himself. He said "hello" and then told me his name. He said, "The two guys sitting at the table in the back are my brothers. You've probably heard of us," and I replied, "No, sir". He then took his wallet out of his back pocket, opened it up and thumbed through what looked like was about $1,000. He then asked me if I knew what that was, referring to the money. I told him that it looked like money. He said, "that's right, but more specifically, it's fine money. You see, my brothers and I like to squirrel hunt. We start hunting about the first week in August, because that is when squirrels normally start cutting nuts and they are easier to find. Our family eats all the squirrels we kill, and we don't sell or waste any. They're really good in Brunswick Stews or even fried. Now if you catch us shooting squirrels out of season or over the limit, we'll pay off the ticket with this money, but you are going to have to be good to catch us."

I thanked him for the information and told him that I would surely be on the lookout for them. I was in Warren County from Oct 1, 1979 until August 1, 1993 and I saw him one time riding his bike down a dirt road lined with hardwoods along Fishing Creek off Baltimore Road south of Warrenton. This particular day he was wearing a 22-caliber handgun holstered on his right hip. It was in early September. I stopped to talk to him and asked if he had seen any squirrels today. I also questioned him about the pistol and he just laughed and said it was for protection.

Now he and his brothers loved to hunt squirrels, and they did so anytime they wanted to, as I mentioned earlier, season in or out. They used to mail squirrel tails to the officer stationed there before me, just to aggravate him. One day they called this officer to Hammes Mill Road, off Baltimore Road, on a hunting violation report. Someone was supposed to be hunting squirrels illegally. The officer was sure hoping it was the three brothers. Now would be his chance to catch them and prove himself. The road was a dead end road that turned off Baltimore Rd about a mile or so south of Warrenton and this caller (we later found out it was one of these brothers) knew from which direction the officer would be coming in. As the officer turned down Hammes Mill Road, he saw something stretched across the road. As he got closer it became clear to him that he had been set up. Stretched across the road and tied to fishing line were squirrel tails.

N.G. Crews, an Officer III at the time and now a sergeant, told me of a time he and another officer caught the three brothers hunting near Arcola. I was told the brothers had a few drinks and decided to go hunting. To spice things up a bit, they put money in a pot and decided that whoever came back with the most meat would win the pot. Crews spotted their car parked by a creek near Arcola and backed his car up and around the curve where they could not be seen. He then sent the officer working with him into the woods to find the three brothers while he watched the vehicle. They didn't have to wait long. As two of the brothers were looking over their kills by their truck, Crews pulled up in his car. One of the boys was missing, however. A little while later the third brother exited the woods several hundred yards from the car and saw what was happening. He was hiding his gun and booty when the other officer approached him from behind, confronted him, picked up the gun and booty and took him to the car. There were a lot of squirrels killed that day, but also found in the back game pouch of the jacket was a fawn deer and some quail — all out of season.

The three brothers were also caught another time by Alton Pridgen. Pridgen was the first game warden in Warren County and when I got there, he had been retired for some time. Any new game warden that came to Warren County had to first go meet Pridgen. So it was my turn to meet the legend. His wife Mattie met me at the door, and we went into the living room area. Alton told me to sit where he could see me. He looked me over a time or two, talked to me for about half a day, and then I had to await his verdict on whether I was going to make it in Warren County or not. I got his approval and before I left, he gave me a couple of things to think about. He said, "Don't ever write a ticket to a person that you wouldn't take yourself, don't ever say anything about a person that you wouldn't say to their face (he also said that I probably wouldn't be able to do that one but that I needed to try,) and treat everyone with respect and be fair to them. You have to work with them, go to church with them and deal with them in their businesses, and you would want to be treated the same way." Sounds like the Golden Rule to me.

Pridgen said that one day he had gotten a report that this person was going hunting in the general area where he would be working. He said that he got there early in the morning, tied a string around a limb of a tree and hid in some brush. As he waited there, every now and then, he would tug on the string and make the leaves shake. After doing this for a while he heard someone tipping through the woods and coming to the tree. He pulled the string one more time and then waited for the hunter to come to him. As one of the brothers was looking up into the tree for the squirrel, Pridgen called out his name and asked for his license. Now that was being caught.

I heard all kinds of wildlife stories from Pridgen, including one about the time the first deer track was spotted in Warren County. Someone found the track in the Inez community and drove back to Warrenton to tell his friends. Inez, NC, was a small crossroad surrounded by farmland at this time about 15 miles south of Warrenton on Highway 58. When he told his buddies, they too, wanted to see it, so they drove back to Inez just to see a deer track. Because there weren't many deer then, there was not nearly as much hunting as there is now. Crews told me that he used to go by the only hardware store that sold hunting licenses and check the list of those that had bought a hunting license. The community was so small that everyone knew everyone else, so knowing who had a license and who didn't was pretty simple. If he saw someone whose name was not on that hunting license list and they were hunting, that person got a ticket. There was no need to check the others.

In the early years, when the Commission was new, the officers in the field had to purchase their own side arms to carry. Pridgen's was a 32-caliber automatic, which he carried in a 45-caliber army holster that had the top flap that snapped on the side. He said that he would open the flap and drop the pistol in the holster. The holster was so large that the pistol nearly went out of sight. To get it out, he had to tilt the pistol holster backwards and dump the pistol out of the holster. So much for quick draw.

One day he was going out to check some hunters and he got Mattie, his wife, to drive him. He sat in the front passenger seat and wore a bonnet on his head, undercover style. This technique took years of practice to perfect, and it also allowed him to get close enough to the hunters so that he could recognize who had a license and who did not. By using this method, he said that he didn't have to chase a hunter as far to catch him, if at all.

That reminds me of the time that Pridgen wanted to patrol with me. I told him that I would pick him up at his house that morning and we would go out together to clean up the county of poachers. We were patrolling near his house and had just driven through Rabbit Bottom,

NC on a road to Hollister. I was driving very slowly and scanning the woods and fields as we talked about things and people he knew in Warren County, really wanting to impress this old-time game warden. I was looking out of my window to the left when I spotted a hunter at the edge of a field, just through a thin patch of woods.

I eased the car to a halt on the right side of the road and got out of the car very slowly and quietly, being careful not to slam the door and risk the chance of being heard and having a chase on my hands (this old game warden trick is still in use today). I jumped the ditch and began to ease around a small field about 75 yards deep. I found what looked like a deer trail into the field and followed it through the woods to another field about 30 yards away, slipping from tree to tree keeping each tree between me and my hunter. I just knew that Pridgen was watching, impressed with my technique, probably remembering the days he was a young tracker like me. As I neared the hunter I stopped. I was as still as a cat waiting to pounce on its prey. Something was wrong. It was then that I realized that I had made a big mistake, a mistake that would probably follow me the next 10 years of my career. I slowly turned around and returned to the car. I got in and didn't say a word as I started to drive off. The next minute or two was very quiet. Finally, Pridgen broke the silence and asked me if the reason I didn't check the hunter was because I knew him? I said, as if I had done this thing a thousand times, "Not exactly, it was a scarecrow." You could hear Pridgen laughing all the way down the road.

It was always kind of interesting to go to Pridgen's house. He was a good man but he sure did like to pick on Mrs. Mattie, in a loving way of course, because he sure loved that woman. Ms. Mattie loved Alton as well. You see it in her eyes and smile every time Alton asked for something. While I was there, he would tell Mattie to go get us a drink or something to eat. He'd tell her to close the blinds, go get his oxygen bottle or the trashcan. Miss Mattie would always be sitting in a chair on the right side of the living room either knitting or asking about Margaret. Pridgen had emphysema pretty bad, and he wasn't expected to last very long. Pridgen knew that and decided that he knew of a way to "beat the system." He would buy a car for him and Mattie. Not just any car but a Cadillac, fully loaded. He would put life insurance on it and when he died, it would be paid for. As little as Mattie drove, that car would last her a lifetime. He would no longer have to worry about her trying to keep the old car up and running. He figured that he would only make about two years' worth of payments and that would be all. So what if they were a little high? The trouble was, that he lived, not only long enough to pay for that car, but almost long enough to pay for another car. Each time I saw him, after he told me that story, he'd bring it up again. That sure got his goat.

November 1984

One morning I was working deer hunting near Bethlehem, NC, near the Halifax and Warren County line.

I was going to work a dog hunting club that I had received some illegal reports about, and I had made my way to that area before daylight and legal hunting time. I hid my patrol vehicle, a Ford Bronco 4X4, in a stand of small pines just tall enough to cover the top of my vehicle. I pulled a large green parachute over my truck to help hide it and then waited. Hunters always have some type of radio to talk to the other guys and keep up with the dogs. Most clubs used modified 40-channel CB radios, meaning their CBs had been altered to not only get the regular 40 channels, but an additional 80 channels below regular CB frequencies and 80 channels above regular CB frequencies. I also had acquired one of these CBs from a friend of mine, who also happened to be a District Court judge. I knew the CB channel of this particular club I was working on, so all I had to do was listen. It wasn't long before the sun started coming up and you could hear the hunters talking on the CB about where to drop the dogs out. I knew the area they were going to hunt and so I got ready.

About an hour into the hunt I heard shots and then one hunter called another and said, "You need to come down here." It was starting to sound good to me, but I sat still. The hunter being called asked where he was. "At the end of the Barn Path, and you need to come now." That sounded like an invitation to me, so I pulled the parachute off of the truck and headed to the Barn Path. I had to go right by the hunting club located on a dead end dirt road, so this had to be fast. As I passed the hunt club I saw a hunter running to his truck and then heard him say over the CB, "Here he co—". It was at this time I keyed the CB and began patting the mike on my thigh, breaking his communication with his friends. Since I was in between the two hunters talking, I was transmitting over their radio traffic. I released the CB microphone key and heard, "What did you say? Someone is transmitting over you." My hunter said, "I said, here comes the——-." and I keyed over the hunter's CB again. Then I saw a group of three or four trucks parked together beside an old barn and I headed that way, FAST.

As I approached them in my vehicle, hunters started walking back to their trucks and started driving off. I zeroed in on one remaining truck parked in the woods and drove straight to it. I got to the truck and saw an orange ball cap on a hunter who was stooped over in some leaves in the woods. As I was running to him I heard over the hunter's CB, "The game warden's here. Ok too late, he got you." I walked to the hunter who was skinning a deer and he never looked up at me in the face but he did tilt his head slightly to look at my polished boots and said, "You got me. How much is this going to cost?" I told him that would be up to the magistrate. The doe season had not come in yet and he had killed a doe deer out of season. I asked for his brand new Browning A5 12-gauge shotgun lying on the ground beside the deer and he asked, "Are you going to take my gun too?" "I sure am and the judge may or may not give it back to you when you show up for court." He said "Man, please don't take my gun. My wife just bought it for me. She's going to kill me."

At court he was found guilty of taking an antlerless deer during the closed season, normally a $100 fine, and given a choice of a $250 fine and losing the gun or $500 fine plus court costs and keeping the gun. He kept the gun.

November 1985

I was patrolling deer hunting in the Embro area about seven miles out of Warrenton and was working my way west about a mile west of the Embro Crossroads. It was about dark, to the point that you almost needed headlights to safely drive, and I saw a truck about a quarter mile in front of me pull out of a woods path and turn my way. As he got closer I turned my headlights on bright to keep him from seeing who I was as I passed him. All Wildlife patrol vehicles had switches that would turn your brake lights, parking lights and back up lights off while working at night, and so I turned my brake lights off. As soon as he passed me, I began slowing down. As he rounded a curve and could not see me anymore, I turned my vehicle around and began to catch up to him blackout. I got behind the truck and just followed him to see what he was doing and where he was going. The truck turned south onto Marmaduke Road and I turned and continued to follow him, still remaining far enough back so as not to seen. Soon I saw the truck pull into a farmhouse and drive around to the back of the house.

I stopped on the dirt road with my lights out next to a hedgerow just across the ditch and just waited for something to happen. I hadn't seen this person do anything illegal; I just had a hunch. Approximately ten minutes later I saw the truck back up to a skinning pole and knew that I had struck pay dirt. I got out of my patrol vehicle and walked to the house, being very careful to stay in the shadows of trees next to the house. I stopped behind one tree and watched the hunter turn on a bright light facing his skinning pole and pull a deer from his truck and hang it on the pole. As the hunter started to skin the deer, I slowly walked to him, again, being careful to keep a tree or something between the hunter and me. I got within fifteen steps of the hunter proudly skinning his deer, got behind the bright light and then called him by name and told him to drop the skinning knife on the ground.

He stopped and looked toward the light he had turned on and dropped the knife. I approached and stated to the hunter, whom I knew really well, "That's a nice deer you got there. Did you get off a clean shot?" He didn't answer but just looked down at the ground. "I guess I need to check your big game tags to make sure they are validated and also see your registration card." He stated "Mangum, I haven't validated my tag or registered the deer." "Ah, don't worry about that," I said. "We can work with that, but did you know that the doe season is not in yet? Doesn't come in until December." "Mangum, I didn't know." "Well, I am going to let you keep the deer since it is skinned, but right now you're under arrest for taking a doe deer during the closed season, failing to tag, failing to register and transporting an unlawfully taken deer." "Damnit, I didn't even hear you coming." "You weren't supposed to," I replied.

Night Deer Hunting (Firelighting)

Firelighting is an illegal method of taking deer at night with a light and weapon. The statute says that, "It is unlawful to display an artificial light in an area frequented by deer between the hours of a half hour after sunset to a half hour before sunrise while having in your possession a firearm or bow and arrow." The fact that you have a firearm or bow and arrow, or whether you know it was loaded or not, is prima facie evidence that you are firelighting deer. This was, and still is, a very dangerous activity to work. First of all, it happens at night and you are usually by yourself in the middle of the county, away from houses. Your nearest help is in the next county — mine being in Roanoke Rapids in Halifax County, approximately 35 miles away — and that officer really didn't know the county like you knew it, with all of the local names for the various state roads. The vehicle that you are stopping probably has more than one person in the vehicle, some of the time drinking. The violators know they are violating the law, could lose their hunting license for two years, pay a minimum $250 fine and court costs, lose their weapons and could lose their vehicle, depending on their attitudes at the time of the stop. On top of that, they will probably be arrested and get a free night in jail.

It is exciting work, but you have to be on top of your game and not make any mistakes. One minute you're lying on the hood of your car next to a soybean field on a cold, clear night. It's quiet and you're lost in your thoughts. A billion stars in the sky. Then it happens. You hear a vehicle coming down the dirt road and you can tell that it is traveling slowly. Maybe you hear the sound of rocks popping as a tire is passing over them. Maybe you hear the muffler of a jacked-up hunting truck rumbling down the road. The vehicle approaches the field and stops on the road. Nothing happens for a moment, and then you see a two million candle power spotlight light up the field, sweeping from one side to the other and finally stopping on a deer. Your heartbeat picks up a little as you're whispering to yourself, "Shoot, shoot." You hear a loud shot and its report echoes through the night air. If you are working with another unit, you call them and shout, "He just shot, come on." If not, you jump off of the hood, pull the parachute off of the car, jump in and take off down the dirt path blackout so you don't spook him.

Your vehicle hits the road and you race to get as close to the violator as possible without him seeing you. You then call in your location to whomever is working that night, turn on blue lights and siren to stop the vehicle, with your heart pounding in your chest. You're thinking of every possible scenario that might happen and what you would do in each case. I would get behind the vehicle as quickly as possible to get the license number. I would then call it in to my dispatcher in Raleigh. As I exited the car, I would tell my dispatcher that I will be out of the patrol vehicle listening for the violator's plate information to be broadcast over the PA system. If I don't respond in five minutes, I tell them to contact the Warren County Sheriff Department with my last known location. I found that when working by myself, if a violator's name and address was broadcast over the PA system, it tended to take a little tension off the situation. Also if anything happened to me, the violator knew that our office, and any other officer working that night, knew who he was.

Now most of the time you worked firelighting, you never saw or heard a thing. These nights, and there were many of them, were lonely, except for mosquitoes when it was hot and very quiet. So to spice them up a bit, I would sometimes go by one of the local hunting clubs to eat supper before I went to my setup. Supper usually consisted of fried venison, potatoes, beans of some type, gravy and corn bread. You could eat all you wanted, and then I would take some fried venison sandwich to snack on later. Of course everyone asked me if I was working that night, and most of the time I would say that I was just getting off work and because it was so late, I thought that I would stop by to eat before going home. Other times I might tell them that I was just going out to work in that area for a while.

After leaving the club, I would move to the other end of the county to work, knowing that I would not be having any problems with that club tonight. Some of the hunters would often go out shining for deer just to draw me out to check them. You could tell what they were up to by how much or how little they shined their lights. Sometimes they would shine every inch of the field and even shine the light in the dark sky just to make sure I saw it. This was a big waste of my time, as I knew that they knew I was in the area, so if I was working in the lower part of the county I would move to the northern portion of the county as far as, sometimes, twenty miles away to work. I would drive to my setup and back the truck in a "hole," a place I had cut into the woods two months earlier to hide my car. I would get a parachute out of the back and throw it over the vehicle to cover the chrome areas just in case someone shined a spotlight in my direction. The parachute made your vehicle blend into the area. Once that was done, I would jump up on the hood of the vehicle and lie on top of the parachute. Now if it was cold, as many nights were, I would get completely under the parachute. The heat from the vehicle would rise from the motor and sometimes lift the parachute up some. The heat would also stay under the parachute a long time, keeping you nice and toasty. Then the long wait would begin.

Depending on the area you chose to work, you may not see or hear anything move all night. Other times, it seemed like everyone and his brother was out shining for deer. You could tell 90 percent of the time who was hunting and who wasn't by what type of light they used and the way they shined the light into the field. As I mentioned, some hunters shined a lot just to see if you were working in that area. Some hunters who were actually out to get a deer would do this to see if you were in the area and would come out to stop them. If you did stop and check them, they would go back the way they came and to a spot where they had hidden a rifle and retrieve it. They would then go to a different part of the county to shoot deer, knowing you were somewhere else working. Sometimes it could be a family out looking for deer to show their kids, especially around Christmas. There were a lot of families out looking for deer around Christmas hoping to see Rudolph. If I stopped one of these vehicles I would always play along, telling the kids that I had just seen him about thirty minutes ago heading the same direction that they were heading.

Because of these types of shining, later in the deer season we would usually not stop any vehicle shining until after 2300. That was the cut off time to legally shine a light looking for deer in most counties in North Carolina. If someone did shine a light looking for deer after 2300 hours, I would search their vehicle for a weapon and if I did not find one, I would issue a citation for a curfew violation or "displaying an artificial light between the hours of 2300 and a half hour before sunrise," if that county had a local curfew law.

The type of light we really looked for was a fast sweeping light across a field. This fast sweeping motion would light up the eyes of a deer in a particular area.

The hunter would then get his gun ready, get as close as he could to the deer in his vehicle and then turn the light on just long enough for his buddy to shoot one of them. Sometimes the driver would drop his buddy out with the carcass so the partner in crime could drag the deer to the road while the driver left the area for an hour or two. If we did not show up to check on the shot we heard, the driver would return and pick up the deer and his partner. Other times, they would just drive around the county shooting the number of deer that they wanted and then come back for them in the morning, when it was legal to shoot deer. The only problem this caused them was when we checked them and they had four deer in the back of the pickup, stiff as boards and with frost on the hides. This would cause the criminals a huge pucker factor trying to explain how a deer could freeze solid in less than thirty minutes. This was also a fun time for a Wildlife Officer, because we knew what they had done and that we were going to charge them, but we just liked to have a little fun asking a lot of questions trying to get the criminal to confess. We usually didn't need the confession, because this type of hunter usually didn't bother to notch their deer tags to record the kill.

Other nights I would stop by one of the pizza places that gave us half-price pizzas, purchase a large all-the-way pizza and carry it to my setup. Lying on top of the patrol vehicle halfway under a parachute, eating a large pizza under a totally cloudless sky was wonderful to me. Sometimes the sky was so clear during the winter months you could see forever and count shooting stars all night long. The only slightly dull spot in the sky was the Milky Way. Also if you used the night vison monocular that was issued to you, the number of stars quadrupled. In the earlier years I was driving a Chevy Blazer 4x4 and then was issued a Ford Bronco 4x4. These vehicles would get you to just about anywhere in the county. They would also get you VERY stuck at times. One of the best things about them was that you could pull into a setup with the front facing the woods in a way that you still had a fast exit, if you needed to stop someone quickly. This way you could lower the back glass and drop the tailgate. This just so happened to make a perfect spot to roll out a sleeping bag to lie on. Using the truck in this position allowed you to still use the parachute over you AND the truck and lay either on it or the sleeping bag.

I remember one of my first firelighting details using the aircraft; I was working with an "old school" supervisor. He was driving and we pulled into our setup and parked the car behind some thick brush. I kind of mentioned that we couldn't see the field we were working from here. With his years of knowledge working with the aircraft, he said we didn't need to see the field, that the airplane would tell us what was happening. He then opened his trunk and drug out an Adam and Eve, two-person sleeping bag. I was a little concerned about this because he owned the sleeping bag and it was his patrol car, so that would make him Adam. He then threw the double sleeping bag on top of the hood of his car, jumped up on the vehicle hood and got under the sleeping bag. He then took out the Commission's Motorola radio and put it on the hood near the windshield between his side and my side. When this was done, he rolled over on his left side facing away from me and pulled the sleeping bag up around his neck. I stood by the front of the car for a while, not comfortable with my "Eve" title and he turned and said, "Are you going to just stand there or get in the bag?" I kind of liked the idea about standing there but it was pretty cold so I sat on the hood of the car, put my legs onto the hood and got under the sleeping bag. I, however, lay flat on my back with hands in the defensive position.

After a few minutes I asked him about the aircraft detail. He said, "They'll call us when they need us." A few minutes later, I heard him snoring. This job was getting better all the time. I lay on the hood of the car for about an hour, trying hard not to go to sleep, but my supervisor's snoring had a sort of soothing, rhythmic pattern to it and the hood of the car was really warm, heating up the sleeping bag. Soon my eyes started to get really heavy. I never really fell into that seventh REM of sleep everyone talks about, but I did manage a little drool out of the right side of my mouth. The radio never let you get to sleep fully, because about every twenty to thirty minutes the plane would fly over your position and ask for your "Sig 1," or area of location. At night when you worked with the plane the observer would ask for a "Sig 12" or give a light to mark your location. It was still a great way to work firelighting, though, and

I must admit, I did use the method that I was taught that evening by my experienced supervisor to work firelighting in the future.

As an observer in the plane flying over the Pamlico Sound in Beaufort County, on a clear night, you could see the city lights from all of the big cities around you. You could see lights from Raleigh (85 miles away) to Cape Hatteras and Cape Lookout Lighthouse (about 80 miles as the crow flies). You could look north and see the lights from Virginia Beach, Va. and south to Morehead City, NC. It was really a neat thing to work as an aircraft observer. So being able to see all of these city lights, imagine what you could see looking through night vision goggles. It was amazing. You could see a man light a cigarette on the ground.

Just about when you thought it would be a quiet night lying on the warm hood of a patrol car in a sleeping bag with your supervisor, the observer would call you out of your sleep, I mean, setup, and start giving you directions to go and turns to take. Most of the time you had no idea where you were going. The pilot would watch the vehicle shining and the observer would pick your car up as it was moving. He would tell you when to turn, what direction and how far the next turn was. He would continually give you an update on the vehicle you were trying to get up with and how far and which direction it was headed. Sometimes the road you were told to turn on would put you headed straight toward the vehicle you were trying to stop. If this happened, the observer would tell you to pull into a dirt path or even a drive way and turn off your lights. The vehicle shining his light would then go by you. You would turn your brake light and parking lights off with a switch under the dash, back out of the path and drive hard, blackout, to catch up with the vehicle. Once you were on his taillights, you would give as much description concerning the vehicle and occupants as you could, without turning your headlights on. Once the information was given to the observer, you would then turn on all lights on your car, including blue lights. This usually scared the pants off of the occupants and was a good way to give you an advantage. Sometimes you would find guns and sometimes (most of the times) not. Guns or not, tt was still an exciting way to make a living.

November 1979

My first firelighting case came on the morning of Thanksgiving, 1979 — my first year with the commission. This would be my first all-night deer hunting detail. Julian Alman came by and picked me up in his dark green Chevy Malibu and we were off to the Harman House setup, which was between Inez and Bethlehem. Sergeant N.G. Crews and Burley Clark would be working in another vehicle about two miles south of us. Julian and I had been set up most of the night, backed into an old woods path, waiting for something to happen. It was about 0400 in the morning when we heard the shot that changed my life. We were outside of the vehicle talking when we heard the shot over our right shoulder, about a half mile away. We knew that it would put the shot on a dead end dirt road called Ernest Turner and that whoever was doing the shooting would have to come by us, if we got to the Turner Road in time. We radioed Crews and Burley and told them that we would be moving to Highway 58 at the corner of the Turner Road. They would be coming in from the Centerville side, south of us. We had just gotten setup again on Highway 58, watching Turner Road, and we could hear a vehicle moving from the direction of the shot toward us. Crews radioed us that they could see the vehicle and was going to make the stop head on at the intersection of Turner Road and Highway 58.

About thirty seconds later they called to tell us that the vehicle had refused to stop for them and was headed our way. We pulled out of our setup and turned left to meet the vehicle and try to stop it head on, but the vehicle swerved to our right, rammed the front of our car, knocking us sideways and smashing the front right side of our vehicle. His vehicle, a blue van, ran into the ditch and back out onto the road. We backed out of the way and let Crews' car come by us, chasing the vehicle. We pulled our car in behind Crews' car. THE CHASE WAS ON! Julian followed Crews, with Crews' car staying back about 100 yards from the van. As we entered a straight-of-way Julian decided, I might add against my better judgment, that he was tired of being the second vehicle and passed Crews' car. Later Julian said that he thought that Crews' car could not keep up with the van, but Crews said that he was just pushing (staying close) to the van and was going to let him make a mistake and wreck. During the chase from Inez to the Highway 43/58 intersection (about 7 miles), we hit speeds of over 100 miles an hour. At one time Julian tried to tap the left rear of the van and the van swerved to the right just as we tapped him. This caused us to go off of the road to the left, across a shallow ditch, up a slight embankment, back across the ditch and back onto the road and we never lost our chase position. By the way, that TOO was against my better judgment.

During the chase we had our Raleigh Dispatcher contact the Warrenton Sheriff Department to let them know that we may be headed their way into town if the van turned left at the next intersection. As we approached the Highway 43/58 intersection, Julian went left of the van as the van began to turn left and did a running road block. Realizing that he could not turn left, the van turned right, south on Highway 43 to Arcola. This maneuver kept the speeding van from going into town and possibly hurting someone. During this stretch of the chase, the van swerved wide left in a curve and ran two trucks pulling boats off of the road, but luckily not into a deep ditch bordering the road. It was also during this stretch of the chase that my right leg began to shake up and down, really bad. I tried to hold it down with my hand but soon gave up. All I could go was to hold on to the dash and give Julian information on the curves coming up. At one point Julian tried to tap the van again with the front of our car but the van hit the brakes, causing us to run into the back of him.

Of course our vehicle's front end was already tore all to pieces so it really didn't matter much to us.

As we were approaching an intersection near Arcola, the road doglegged to the right. We were behind the van about fifty yards and saw a person in the vehicle throw an object out of the driver's window. The object hit the asphalt road, causing sparks. Julian and I saw this at the same time but he reacted first by grabbing his Wildlife Protector Guide book and throwing it out of his window to mark that spot. Papers went everywhere, and we knew that wouldn't be hard to find. All during this time the chase never stopped. In fact, I think it got faster. Over the next several miles we stayed on the violator's tail. I sort of knew the area, and I told Julian we were coming up on an intersection at the Essex crossroad. We were still running hard and suddenly the van hit his brakes hard, causing us to run into the back of him again. This slowed our pursuit but also put us into a sideways slide that luckily caused our vehicle to straddle an asphalt median, minus one recently knocked down stop sign, thanks to the van in front of us. On impact, our vehicle pushed the van straight through the intersection, across another median, across a service station parking lot, (where it destroyed a large swinging oil sign,) and back out onto Highway 43 with us dead on his tail.

As we hit the highway again, our dome light fell from the ceiling, turned itself on, and began swinging all around the car as if it were a miniature lighthouse trying to warn others of danger. Not needing this additional stress, I pulled the light from the ceiling, wires and all. While I was working on our lighting situation, Julian had regained our position behind the van and continued the chase. About three miles outside of Essex on Highway 43, the van started to slow down and then pulled to the right side of the road. We were going so fast to catch up, and this happened so suddenly, that we went right by the stopped van to his left about a hundred yards and had to back up to the front of the van, keeping it from attempting to leave again. We bailed out of our car and ran back to the van.

When we got there, Burley already had the barrel of his Colt Trooper 357 Magnum stuck in the left cheek of the driver. Seeing that this person was under complete control, we went to the passenger side of the van and met Crews coming up the embankment with his suspect. The passenger had bailed out of the van and fallen down an embankment of kudzu, tripping as he tried to run. Crews said that he had to dive on him to stop him. As we reached the front of Crews' car, which was at the back of the van, Burley gave me his "prisoner" and told me to frisk and hold him at the front of Crews' car. Not knowing exactly what to do, having only been on the job for about seven weeks, I bent him over the front of the hood and held his head on the hood. I also had his left arm in an arm lock behind his back, all the while feeling for objects that may be in his pockets or waistband with my free hand. When Julian came up a short time later to assist me, he said that I had the man's left arm up around his right ear. I guess I was a little pumped up.

We had the van towed in and stored for court and took the two men to the magistrate's office, where we finished up our paperwork. We had found their deer in the back of the van, which sported a personal license plate that read "Sh—1," and moved the deer carcass into the trunk of Julian's car. We found out later that the van, which included all of the "extras," had been featured in van and car shows. It was a shame that the deer was bleeding all over the blue carpet in the back of that fancy van.

Now it was time to eat breakfast. We drove Julian's wrecked car, with the deer and blood all over the trunk, to my house in Warrenton and left it there. We drove my car to a restaurant on Main Street in Warrenton and started to unwind on sausage and eggs while we relived the chase. After breakfast we returned to my house. My in-laws were up from Beaufort for a Thanksgiving visit and everyone was standing around Julian's car — the front end was tore all to pieces, a dead deer and blood all over the trunk. I didn't go into great detail because I didn't want my wife to worry about me from then on. I just told them that it had been a busy night.

A week or so later, Burley talked with the passenger of the van, who lived in Louisburg, NC. He told Burley that the driver was his cousin from Washington, D.C., and his cousin had tried to get him to open the back doors of the van and shoot at us, but he refused. What was a bad chase could certainly have been a lot worse.

A GAME WARDEN'S ADVENTURE

December 1979

I was sitting at the house on Reid Circle in Warrenton, and at about 2200 hours I received a call from a concerned landowner that someone was shooting deer at night just down the road from his house. The vehicle I was driving at the time was a green 1974 Jeep Cherokee, three speed on the floor, with a blown head gasket. That Jeep sounded like a tractor without a muffler, but I didn't care. It was my patrol vehicle. Anyway, the landowner gave me the directions to the "shots fired" area, and I made a beeline to Fate Weaver Road. I entered the road from the south, off of State Road 1001, and stopped and turned off the engine to see if I could hear anything. A heavy thunderstorm was approaching from the southwest, and although there was no rain yet, the wind was blowing hard and plenty of lightning was coming my way. I decided that I would try, as best as possible, to ease down the road blackout and hopefully find my shooter. I drove down the road about a mile and came to a sharp left curve in the road. As I made the turn in the road, I noticed a bright light coming from behind an old home place that had burned down and fallen in.

I backed up, turned right into the driveway and idled forward until I saw a Coleman lantern hanging from a huge oak tree behind a pickup truck with a camper top. The light illuminated the whole area. I left my motor running, with headlights on, got out of the car and started to make my way around the left front of my vehicle. When the headlights of my vehicle were shining on my right thigh, I looked up to see a silhouette of a man beside the truck and a double barrel shotgun pointed at me. My thought process slowed and what seemed like ten minutes really turned out to be about a minute. My first thoughts were very slow and methodical, "I could draw my weapon and fall down behind my left front tire for cover, but I think he could shoot me first. I could try to draw my weapon and dive to the left, but he would shoot me first. I could tell him that I was a game warden, but if he is violating the law he might shoot me." Nothing I was thinking seemed to have a good ending, so I went with my best choice as I slid my hand slowly to my weapon. "State Wildlife Officer, lower your shotgun". The next thing I heard was, "DAMN man, I'm sorry," as he lowered his shotgun. "I thought you were some guys I ran off earlier coming back to pay me a visit, only this time it sounded like they were driving a tractor with no muffler."

The gentleman proceeded to tell me that he and his wife were from Virginia and he was a retired trooper. They came down to camp out on their family's home place lot. When they had backed in to park their truck, a car pulled into the driveway, with about four guys in it, playing loud music. "I told them to leave, but they just sat in the car looking at us. I picked up my shotgun and fired two rounds in the air and they took off. I thought you were those guys coming back for trouble." I assured him that although I may have sounded like them, I most definitely was not. I told him of the report that I had received earlier. He said that the shots the landowner had heard and reported were probably the two shots that he had fired into the air. He apologized several more times and offered me food, drinks, beer, just about anything he had. I thanked him for the offer but decided that I had better head home and check my pants. We shook hands and I left to meet the landowner who called in the report to let him know what I had discovered. I remember thinking that night, "I need a quieter patrol vehicle."

November 1983

One night I was working a firelighting report on the dirt portion of Earnest Turner Road, about four miles north of the Franklin/Warren County line. This dirt portion of road was a dead end section, and there was one hunting club located at the very end. I was set up in a small field and had my parachute over the patrol vehicle to keep from being seen too easily. I had waited to arrive at my set up until after 2300 because of the curfew law, which doubled my chances of catching someone who would be intentionally trying to violate the law and shoot a deer at night. Sometime around midnight, I was lying on the hood of my patrol vehicle, under the parachute because of the cold air, and just enjoying the peace and quiet of a cold night in a very desolate area. I remember it was very clear that night.

All was quiet when suddenly I heard a loud report of a gun coming from directly behind me, putting the shot in Franklin County, as my setup was very close to Shocco

Creek, the boundary line for the Franklin and Warren County line. I took out my county map and aligned the map, as best I could, in the northerly direction to give me some idea of where the shot may have come from. I noticed a loop road located off of Highway 561 in Franklin County, Wood Church Road, which had a dead end road running north in my direction. This was Thomas Jones Road, and my first road to check. I secured my parachute in the trunk and headed to my suspect road. As the crow flies the distance was only about one to one and a half miles, but it was six miles by road so I had to move quickly. I pushed the patrol vehicle hard up Turner Road and turned on Highway 58 south to Frankin County. When I got to Highway 561, I turn left and ran hard to Wood Church Road.

Once there I stopped, turned off the motor and got out of the vehicle to listen. I heard another shot exactly the way I was heading, jumped back in my vehicle and continued my hunt. When I got to within a half mile of Thomas Jones Road, I began slowing down, first, because of the noise my vehicle would be making riding on a rock dirt road and, second, if anyone was down this road he would have to come by me in his vehicle to leave the area. I turned off all lights on my vehicle, including the brake, parking and backup lights, and continued down the dirt road very slowly blackout. Thomas Jones Road ended, and I saw a dirt path by moonlight on my left hand side. I got out of the vehicle and used my flashlight, half covered, and looked at the dirt path. I noticed a couple sets of tire tracks on the path and was hoping that I made it here in time. I could see an opening in the woods indicating a field about 100 yards in front of me, and I started walking to the field. I stopped at the edge of the field, stooped down and just looked and listened. It was very quiet, and I didn't see anything moving or see any type of light in the field.

Suddenly I heard a VERY loud shot about twenty yards from me along the wood line. I thought I had been shot at. I dove behind a tree and started to pull my service weapon when I noticed a silhouette against the sky that looked like a metal pole. I turn my flashlight on the object and realized I had been tracking a gas cannon. A gas cannon, or propane cannon, is a device fueled by propane and designed to fire a loud report to scare off birds, deer and other predators from a crop or other area. It is fired through a regulator that can be set to fire on a timer from one or two minutes up to about about thirty minutes. I had never seen or heard of a gas cannon before that night. I was disappointed that I did not catch what I thought was a night deer hunter, REALLY happy I was not shot at, and chalked that night up to a training experience. After all, I tracked a shot I heard at night over six miles by road and came within twenty yards of my source.

December 1983

Julian and I loved to work together. We had a lot of good times, including eating a whole BIG jar of pickled devil eggs one morning and then having to work all day with each other (Man, what a day that was!), meeting near Bullocksville State Park in Vance County, building a small fire in the middle of a dirt road and having five hotdogs, buns and mustard for lunch and trying to eat a bushel of oysters together for lunch in our patrol boat. That day didn't turn out as good as some of the others. While trying to open an oyster with a homemade oyster knife we had made out of rebar and a grinder at the State Parks Maintenance Building, Julian's knife slipped off of the oyster and he stuck it into the meaty portion of his hand just under his thumb about an inch. He looked at me and said, "I think we need to go to the emergency room for some stitches," and me, being a caring friend, said, "OK, but let me finish my oysters first." I made him wait only a minute or two and then fussed at him for making me miss my lunch, of course all in fun.

Julian and I knew each other's weaknesses, and we picked on each other a lot, sometimes even "counting ribs." One night he and I were working in the Vicksboro area, on the Warren and Vance County line, and we were parked behind a church. This was the only setup we could find in that area. We had gotten a report that some young boys were shooting deer in a field behind this church, and that night was going to be the night to catch them. We sat there most of the night, occasionally seeing a truck or car come by and shine a field across the street from the church, but nothing looked good enough to stop. If we stopped everything that came by, the word would get out that we were working in that area and we would blow our chances of catching the violators. Anyway, the night was passing by pretty slow. Luckily, Julian had brought a handheld electronic baseball game to pass the night away. We must have played that game for two hours before we decided to see who was the "goosiest."

Julian was kind of touchy when someone touched him in the side. He'd jump and swing his arms back and forth like he was swatting at a bunch of flies. And holler? He sounded like a BUNCH of schoolgirls. He'd jump up and down, flailing his arms back and forth and hollering, just because someone poked him in the side with their finger. He was dangerous! And he DID hate a snake. Anyway, somehow or another I talked him into seeing which one of us was the "goosiest." Now I know this might sound just a tad bit stupid, and maybe even slightly childish, but we were bored to death. To find this out, we decided to count one another's ribs and see who could get to the highest number of ribs before the "countee" laughed. In good faith, I went first. Julian started at the bottom on my rib cage and stuck his finger into my side. He would then roll his index finger over each one of my ribs and working his way up. After about a count of four or five, I was laughing so hard I had to pee, and I hollered for him to quit. I held the pee though, knowing I would be the "counter" next. I started at the bottom of his rib cage and very methodically and intently counted each rib with my index finger. He started twisting and shaking like he was being tortured. He started laughing and then I started laughing, and we were both laughing so hard we were crying. We noticed that it was starting to get bright outside and looked up to see a car with three boys in it sitting right in front of our car with their headlights shining right into our faces. We tried to quit laughing but couldn't. We just sat in our car with the motor off and turned on the blue light to make the car stop. We both got out of our car, still laughing with tears coming down our faces, walked up to the stopped car and asked the boys if they had a gun in the car with them. They said no, and after a brief inspection of the passenger area, we laughed our way back to our patrol car. Needless to say, our night of working was about over. Every time we thought about "counting ribs" we'd start laughing and decided that we probably needed to call it a night.

The following weekend Julian and I decided that we'd get together, go by Afton Gun Club and get some supper and then go to our setup at the old schoolhouse in the Inez area. The schoolhouse was located on Highway 58 at the corner of the Ernest Turner Road. This area was one of my "hot spots" for catching night deer hunters. The club was feeding (cooking) on a Sunday night, and so we thought we'd get some food, take it to our setup and work an "all-nighter." J.J, the club president, was always cooking something at the clubhouse, and we were always invited to eat. That night it was fried venison, string beans, boiled potatoes and biscuits. We talked to the hunters at the club for a while and then made up a couple of plates to take with us, really stacking the venison up, knowing it was going to be a long night. After thanking J.J. we headed to our setup, which was about four miles away. It was an old school house about eight hundred yards off of Highway 58 from Centerville to Warrenton. Also the place was haunted, that being a later story. When we arrived at our Sig 1, I got out of the car and moved to the driver side front of the vehicle, sat my plate on the hood of the car and got ready for a feast. Julian opted to stay in the car to eat his food. We had just started to eat and I heard a shot just north, about a mile from us. I looked at Julian and Julian looked at me and then I saw Julian do something just plain stupid. With his plate in his left hand, he threw his plate, food and all, over his left shoulder into the back seat area. This area covered pretty much the WHOLE back seat from door to door. I mean there was food everywhere. I wrapped my plate up, jumped in the car, LAID my plate on the back seat and sped down the schoolhouse driveway to the highway. The whole time I was driving we were hollering at each other about the food in the back seat. We turned and headed north to the area that I thought the shot came from. We hid our vehicle in some small pines trees and got out of the vehicle to listen for any cars moving. After about an hour or two of dead silence, we decided to drive back to our original setup and sit tight, hoping that whoever had shot would come to our area and shoot again. When we got back, I stepped out of the car to survey the damage to the back seat. It wasn't really bad. A little venison in the back glass, Heinz 57 on the backrest, potatoes on the floor and a biscuit on the arm rest. We salvaged what we could and then split the plate that had been saved and my half eaten plate between us.

At about 2300 hours, we were sitting on the hood of the car and noticed movement on the road off to our right on Turner Road. This movement turned out to be a local resident riding his bike heading toward the intersection. We could hear him saying something, but we couldn't quite make out what it was. He got to the intersection and turned to the left, heading south on Highway 58, still making this moaning sound. We both watched this lone rider on a bicycle, by the glow of the moon, turn into the schoolhouse driveway heading toward us. This time we could make out, "Oiney", "Oiney". He kept saying this over and over. We couldn't help but laugh because it was VERY obvious by his bicycling skills he was intoxicated, severely. He continued to ride his bike by the school but on the opposite side from us, and then into the woods to the location of an old house. I had always thought that the house was abandoned but it turned out that this was where this man lived. We also surmised that "Oiney" must have been his girlfriend or wife. Whoever it was, he seemed to be a little upset over her as we could hear him over and over as his voice faded off into the woods, very slow and drawn out, "Oiney, Oiney, Oiney".

November 1983

I had received a report of firelighting along the Virginia and North Carolina line along Interstate 85. I knew this area pretty well. There was one small dirt path that went through some big water holes from the

Virginia side traveling south along a small creek. This path, which led to one lone soybean field, was hardly ever traveled from the Virginia side but had a good path entering the field from the North Carolina side, which is the one the farmer used. I met with my Sergeant that evening, and we drove my Chevrolet Impala up Interstate 85 north and into Virginia and got off on the first exit. The path I was looking for was seldom used and traveled behind the Virginia Welcome Center. Once I found it, we slowly proceeded to my setup over large rocks and through some deep water holes on the path to the field. Once there, I backed into some woods (where I had recently clear a space big enough for my vehicle with my machete,) threw the parachute over the vehicle and we began our watch. At approximately 2330 hours we saw a four-door older model sedan enter the field from the same direction as we had traveled, from the Virginia side. The vehicle was driving very slowly, and as he went by our setup I told my Sergeant that I was going to walk behind the car to stay close to him and I wanted him to follow me blackout.

Suddenly the car stopped and the driver stuck a Q-beam light out of the driver's window, pointed it over the car top to the passenger side and swept the field looking for deer. I squatted down behind his car and waited. He put the light back into the car and continued his slow pace along the edge of the field. When the driver reached the end of the field, he turned his car to the right and shined his headlights into the field. I still waited, hoping to see him pull the gun out to shoot at something, anything. Unfortunately there was nothing in the field to shoot, so the driver began backing his car to turn around and go out the same way he came in. I called my partner and told him to come up and make the stop using his blue lights. When our car came to a stop and the blue lights had activated, I reached for his car door handle. I pulled the driver door open and hollered, "State Wildlife Officer, turn the car off!"

What happened next kind of surprised me. The driver screamed like a girl and jumped out of the car to run, but I was in his way. I pulled my weapon and told him to stop. He yelled, "I have to piss." I thought to myself, "No you don't, you just pissed all over yourself and the car seat," and boy did he ever. Not seeing any type of weapon I followed him to the woods, about five yards away, to cover him and to see if he was hiding anything. As I watched the driver, my partner searched the car for a weapon but did not find any. I got the driver back to the car and asked why he ran to the woods and he just said, "You scared the hell out of me." I told him that I had good and bad news. "The good news is I am not going to arrest you, and the bad news is, I am going to issue a citation to you for displaying an artificial light after the hours of 2300 hours and before sunrise." This was a violation of a local law to keep hunters from shining Q-Beam spotlights all night and bothering landowners and livestock or chicken houses. Had he had a weapon of any kind he would have been arrested for firelighting deer.

December 1985

In Warren County you could shine a light in search of a deer up until 2300 hours, but from 2300 to a half hour before sunrise you could not shine a light. This was a local law; not all counties had what was known as a curfew law. In some counties a person could not shine a light in search of deer anytime. So after 2300 our night activity got very scarce, and working was a little dull. Most people had gone in for the evening, but not all. Working all night was tough. After about 0100 your eyelids would become extremely heavy and you would start to doze off, a lot. Julian decided that we would take two-hour shifts sleeping and then switch off with each other. The designated sleeper could lie in the back seat and sleep (or try to). When it was my turn in the back seat, I crashed hard. I was tired. I felt like I had just shut my eyes when I heard someone calling me. I opened my eyes, sat up in the back seat and gazed out the front windshield. I saw a car on Turner Road traveling west, and then I felt the heat of a Q-Beam spotlight hit me in the face. It was so bright that it blinded me momentarily. I hollered to Julian, "Did you see that? He just shined me right in the eyes." Julian said something like, "Are you crazy? There isn't anything out there." I rubbed my eyes and the vehicle was gone. I swore to Julian that I saw a vehicle moving but sure enough, there was dead silence outside, and definitely nothing moving. I sat there more than just a little puzzled over what had happened and then realized that as I sat up, Julian had his Maglite in his right hand and had turned his flashlight on approximately 2 inches from my face. I was blind as a bat for about forty-five minutes, as I had lost my night vison from the light. I poured a cup of coffee, got a venison biscuit out of my bag and began my watch.

January 1985

On this night I had chosen to work an area on Rabbit Bottom Road just down the road from the Harmon House, an old plantation with tall white columns in the front and four chimneys coming from the roof. Man, if that house could talk. Beautiful old home. Anyway, there was a cut soybean field right across the road from this old home with a path to the right of the field. As you drove into the field, the path made a couple of turns and ended up at an old barn that had fallen in. In front of the barn and beside the field was a huge, thick hedgerow of bushes, and this was to be my setup for the night. I turned the patrol vehicle to face the road from behind the bushes and got on the hood to begin my long night. It was about 2130 so if anyone shined, I would have a violation. Tonight I decided that I would not put the parachute over the vehicle, because my vehicle was behind some bushes. This one decision could have been fatal. It was cold, so I got into my sleeping bag but left my head out so I could see the field better. I had been sitting there watching this field for about two hours when I heard a vehicle coming from the east, out of Halifax County into Warren County.

I watched as the vehicle, an old model car, turned into the path, stopped, backed out, turned so his headlights swept the field and then pulled back into the path and just sat there, with its lights on me. I watched the car for about ten minutes when, suddenly, I saw a pair of legs cross the headlights of the car from the driver side to the passenger side. I thought this might be the landowner. so I figured I had better go talk to him. I thought about walking to him and reconsidered, thinking that if I did that my setup would be blown for the night. I decided to drive to him and then leave the area. I started my vehicle and pulled to the car blackout and about a hundred yards from the car, I turned on my headlights. I couldn't believe what I was seeing. There was an elderly man with a shotgun in his hand, and when I spotted him he ran as fast as he could back to the car and jumped in. I raced to his car in my vehicle and activated the blue lights to stop him from backing out onto the road. When he stopped backing, I told him over the PA to turn his headlights and his motor off, which he did. I told him to put his hands on the dash of his car and keep them there.

I walked to the car and saw an older woman in the passenger seat and a young boy, about five or six years old, in the back seat. I shined my flashlight on the man and asked, "What are you doing?" He hung his head and said in a low voice, "Some friends told me that there were deer in this field and I came to kill one. I saw what looked like deer eyes in the hedgerows and I was walking up to shoot into the bushes to kill a deer." I said, rather sternly, "That was me on my vehicle. You could have killed me." "I know. I am so sorry. I just needed some meat." Now this was one of those times when I actually believed the person. I said, "I could lock you up, take your gun and seize the car, but from the looks of things, I believe what you are telling me. I've got to write you up but instead of the other charges, I'll just cite you for a curfew violation. If you need deer to eat, I'll bring you some deer. Don't EVER do this again". Following this incident, I brought the old man about three deer that I had seized from hunters who had killed them illegally, one from the current year and two the next year. This would not be the last time I brought someone meat to eat, as there were a lot of poor people in Warren County.

About a week after this happened, I saw a truck shining a light after 2300 hours on Rabbit Bottom Road near the Harmon House and pulled in behind him. I followed him about two miles blackout to see if he would find something to shoot, but he didn't. I turned on the blue light and pulled the truck over. After speaking with the driver, who was alone, I searched his truck for a weapon but did not find one. I issued him a citation for a curfew violation, he thanked me and I walked back to my car. I noticed that the engine was not running and my headlights looked a little dim from being left on. As the truck pulled away, I tried to start my vehicle but all it would do is make the headlights go darn near out and when I let go of the ignition key, the lights would get bright again. I was trying to process what I was going to do next when I noticed the gentleman I had just issued a citation to backing up to me in his truck. He backed up beside me, rolled down his window and said, "Need a jump?" "Well yeah, I guess I do," I replied. "I shouldn't do this but you were so nice about the ticket, I'll help you out." All I could say was, "Thank you." I've often wondered if the way I treated the elderly man with the shotgun, earlier in the week, had anything to do with me getting a jump for my vehicle that night. Kindness for kindness?

January 1988

One night in January of 1988 I was working on State Road 1521, south of Littleton running almost to Arcola. I had set up with my parachute over the patrol vehicle, with me under it, and I remember it was really cold that night. It had been sleeting off and on most of the afternoon and evening, making the roads very slick, so that night I had to be very careful following a vehicle blackout. Sometime after midnight, I heard a vehicle heading south and coming by my setup, which was next to a field about 300 yards from SR 1521. As the vehicle approached the field it began to slow down and then came to a stop. A light came from the passenger window and shined on the field I was watching; the hunter was looking for deer to shoot. I knew I had a curfew violation now, but I wanted to see if he was up to something else.

Since he didn't see any deer in the field, the vehicle, an older model pickup, stopped shining and began traveling south again. I pulled up from my setup and got behind the truck to follow it. I was approximately fifty yards from the back of the truck at this time. We rode by two little fields and nothing happened, and then he turned to the right onto another road. Approximately a half mile down this road, the vehicle slowed and again came to a stop and shined his light out of the passenger window. This time I radioed my dispatcher and gave her my location, license plate number, color of vehicle and the number of occupants I could see through the back window of the truck. I told my dispatcher that I was beginning the vehicle stop and asked her to give me one minute before she gave me the vehicle owner information. That information would be broadcast over the PA system for everyone within shouting distance to hear, including the occupants of the truck. I turned on my blue light and the truck stopped in the middle of the road. As I was approaching the truck, the vehicle information was given over the PA.

I walked to the driver's side and called the driver by the name I had been given by my dispatcher, which startled him some, and asked him if they had seen any deer tonight. He stated that they had seen a few. I asked him if he knew what time it was and, of course, he said he had not been paying the time much thought and that it was probably close to 2300 hours. I said that he was about two hours off; it was closer to 0100. He said that he was sorry and he would stop shining and head straight back to the house. I asked both the driver and passenger to step from the truck and move to the truck's headlights and told them that I needed their identification. I then call my dispatcher and told her both occupants' names and asked the driver if there were any guns in the truck. The driver replied, "Oh shit. I went hunting today and forgot to take my gun out of the truck." I told him, "That's not a problem, I'll get it for you." The rifle was in the front seat on the right side of the passenger, between the seat and the door, loaded. I unloaded the rifle, placed it in the trunk of my vehicle and told the driver that the two of them were under arrest for firelighting deer. I frisked and handcuffed the passenger and put him in the back of my vehicle. Since I had both identifications, I asked the driver to pull his truck off the road onto a dirt path so that could get it after we met with the magistrate.

The driver turned onto the dirt path, put the truck in park, stepped out of the truck and TOOK OFF running into the woods. Knowing how desolate the area was, how far he was away from home and how cold it was, I calmly walked back to my patrol vehicle and picked up the PA microphone. I said, "Hey Johnny (not his real name). It's kinda cold outside, how much longer do I have to wait for you?" I heard nothing. I called out again "Johnny, if you don't come out of the woods, I am going to have your truck towed and you'll be walking home tonight and I'll come by your house on Mulberry Lane tomorrow to arrest you." Still nothing. I then contacted the Warren County Sheriff's Department and made

Turkey trap baited with corn found at Lake Gaston 1985

sure that "Johnny" could hear what I was saying over the PA. I gave the Sheriff's Department my location and the type of vehicle, along with the license plate number. The dispatcher said that a wrecker would be notified and on the way to me shortly. I got back on the PA and told "Johnny" that the wrecker was on the way and that I hoped he made it home okay and did not freeze to death. About two minutes had passed and I heard someone yell to me that he was coming out. When I saw him, I asked if he was all right. "Johnny" walked back to my patrol vehicle and said, "Man, I'm sorry about running. I had to take a crap BAD. You stopping us really tore my stomach up." I asked if he was ready to go to the magistrate's office so we could wrap this night up and go home and he said, "Yes sir." I said, "Okay, turn around so I can put this set of handcuffs on you." "Alright man, let's go. Hey will you help me out in court and tell the judge how cooperative I was?" I replied, "Sure man, I'll help you out". I cancelled the wrecker.

Hunting
January 1985

I loved to see the deer season come in, but I was equally glad to see the deer season go out. We still needed to work night hunting but not nearly as much as we did during the deer season. I loved working small game hunting in Warren County. Warren County had a good quail population, but few young hunters ever hunted them because it was too much work to walk through straw fields or cut overs loaded down with "hawk claw" briars or kill a bird next to a heavily infested briar hedgerow and then have to go into the briars to get him. Very few young hunters used dogs for hunting, but the older hunters did. And it was a joy to watch the bird dogs work. Hearing a pack of beagles chase a rabbit like the world was on fire, then seeing them come into view as they were only walking or trotting along, was also a lot of fun to watch. Most of the older hunters had gotten where they didn't care if they killed a rabbit or not. They just loved to hear the dogs work.

On this particular day I saw where a truck that had pulled into a field path and parked near a wood line in Soul City, NC. I stopped my truck, got out and just listened for any kind of hunt that might be going on. Not hearing anything, I guessed that my hunters were squirrel hunting and so I walked to the wood line and headed into the woods. I walked very slowly, trying to be very quiet. About every twenty to twenty-five yards or so I would stop beside a tree, listening for sounds and scanning the woods very slowly looking for movement. I repeated this tactic until I finally heard a 22-rifle shot about seventy-five yards ahead of me. I walked very quietly until I saw an older gentleman and a young boy squirrel hunting. Each time they would turn their head away from me and walk, I would walk toward them a little faster than their stride, again, keeping a tree between me and the hunters. I stopped moving when they stopped moving and leaned against a tree. I had finally gotten to within about twenty-five steps from them and I heard the older gentleman say something that made me sick. He said, "There's the nest, son. Just shoot into the nest and when that squirrel comes out, shoot him again." I said "Sir. Teaching a young boy to violate the law, just so he can kill something, is not the right way to teach him to hunt. You know it is against the law to shoot into a squirrel nest." The gentleman said, "Man, you scared me half to death! You're right though, and I'm sorry." I said, "I should write you a ticket for this but since he didn't shoot into the nest, I won't. You need to be more responsible than this. And just so you know, if I ever catch you doing this again, you won't get a ticket, you'll be going to jail." "Son," I told the boy,

"Squirrel hunting is a lot of fun, especially when you do it the right way."

September 1, 1986

On this day my sergeant and I, with two more officers, wanted to work one of our largest dove hunts undercover. This hunt was in northern Warren County off of Oine Road. It was a large farm planted in sorghum and corn. The farmer would get the corn up and then bush hog the sorghum field, and the birds loved it. We met at the courthouse in Warrenton, got into a couple of pickup trucks and headed to the dove hunt. When we got into the area, we stopped the trucks on the road and just watched and listened to determine from which area the most shots were being fired. Once we determined that, we drove into the field and set up next to some hunters. We got our chairs out and set them next to the truck, got drinks and started talking really loud like we were somebody. It was a sunny day, not too hot, which is unusual for the first of September in Warren County, and the birds were flying pretty good. I suddenly heard the guys next to us holler, "bird, bird, bird," and we got ready. The bird appeared and I pulled my shotgun up. As it got closer, I fired three times well ahead of the bird, completely missing it, and the guys next to us fired one time and dropped the bird. This was my routine the rest of the day, I would fire and miss, and the guys next to us would knock the bird down. This went on until we had counted at least fifteen birds apiece, putting them over the limit of twelve birds per hunter.

We gathered our gear and put everything back in the truck. Then we got into our truck, rode over to our neighbor's truck, got out and asked them how they were doing. We said we couldn't hit anything. One man stated he had killed forty-one birds and the other man said he had gotten thirty-six birds. We complimented them on their fine shooting skills and asked if we could see the birds. We had never seen that many birds in one spot before. Chests puffed out, both of them took us to the back of the truck and opened their cooler. Yep, looked to be about seventy-seven birds all right. We asked the guys where they were from and one stated, "Florida." I said, "That's a long way from here. Do you have to have a hunting license in Florida?" One man replied, "Sure, you do." "Well, you have to have a license here too, and we're game wardens here in Warren County. Could we see your North Carolina License?" For a second there was complete silence, and then they both started talking at the same time, telling me that they stopped shooting at twelve birds and that all the other birds were given to them. They were sportsmen, they said, and would never shoot over the limit. I thanked them for their concern for wildlife and then asked to check their shotguns for plugs. Again, silence. "How much is this going to cost us?" they finally asked. "Will you help us out in court?"

September 5, 1998

It was the opening day of the dove season. Our work area had planned a big dove detail in Greene County utilizing five officers – Marshall Myers, Milton Jones, Gordon Hobbs, Lt. Rick Venable and myself. We met at 11:30 in Ayden at Bum's Barbecue for lunch. The season began at noon, but there really wasn't any need to start work right at the legal hooting time because the hunters would not have had time to get into the fields and start shooting doves. Besides, Bum's had some of the best barbecue in the area. After a meal of barbecue, Brunswick stew and cornbread, we headed out to some of the larger hunts in Greene County. Gordon and Rick were together, with Gordon's dog (he is our K9 officer). Marshall, Milton, and myself were in Marshall's 1999 Durango. We also had the four-wheeler with us to cut down on some of our walking. One of the first hunts we hit was at Tommy Dail's. He always had a big paid hunt with approximately 100 to 150 hunters, and we wanted to check that hunt while we were still fresh.

We entered the field with the Durango, and I dropped Milton Jones off with the four-wheeler. It would be his job to skirt the outside boundaries, checking for hunters, while those of us on foot would check the middle. As it worked out, I walked up on three hunters sitting on the ground next to a drainage ditch, said some pleasantries and asked to check their guns to make sure they were plugged. The law required that when hunting migratory birds with a shotgun, the shotgun had to have a plug in the magazine making it incapable of holding more than three shells. The first man to my left handed me his shotgun; I checked it for a plug and then checked his license, finding everything in order. I looked at the gentleman in the middle but he made no move to hand me his gun, so I took the shotgun from the gentleman on the far right. After checking his gun and license, I again looked at the gentleman in the middle. He made no move to me, nor would he even look at me. I started to get excited. I reached down, picked up the gun lying beside him and asked for three shells. He looked up slowly and said, "You tell me whose gun it is." Being all knowing I replied, "It's going to be mine if no one claims it." He didn't particularly like my response, but he did hand me three shells. I began putting shelling in the magazine tube and after four shells, I racked one shell into the chamber and asked for a fifth shell, knowing that it too would go into the magazine. I shook my head and asked for the gentleman's hunting license and driver's license.

Examining the driver's license, I saw that the man was from New York City. Since a non-resident that is cited for a violation after crossing the state line cannot be pursued in another state, I called Gordon Hobbs, told him what I had found and asked him to come to my location for a transport to the magistrate's office. I turned to the gentleman I was dealing with and told him that he was under arrest for hunting migratory birds with a shotgun capable of holding more than three shells. The other two men that he was with began to get a little agitated and said to me, "You mean you're going to arrest a man for an unplugged shotgun?" Having been set up for something that I have always wanted to say and not wanting to miss that opportunity, I replied, "No sir, I'm going to arrest him because he is from New York City." The two men looked a little stunned and replied "New York City?" so I explained to them our policy for handling non-residents. To ease the tension a little, I also told the men that they could follow Gordon to the magistrate's office and pick up their friend as soon as we were done with him. That way he would not have to spend any time in jail waiting for someone to bail him out. New York City! I have always wanted to say that.

September 2001

Every officer in my area wanted to work dove hunting near their homes on the Labor Day weekend. The problem was, our captain wanted all of the officers in each area to only work the big dove hunts and check a lot of people. There really wasn't anything wrong with this thinking, because usually the more people you checked, the better the chances of detecting violations. But after five and six years of checking the same hunts year after year, the hunters knew where we would be working on the opening day of dove season. One year I decided, after an annual request from this particular officer, to assist him in working dove hunting in his own work area. This officer knew where the hunt would be, knew most of the hunters that would be there, and most importantly knew their reputations. These hunters liked to get to a field early to watch the flight pattern of the birds. At 12:00, the starting time for shooting birds, each one would walk to the spot they thought was the best. In order to work these hunters for early shooting, unplugged shotguns and over the limits, we had to be in place, hidden, long before they arrived at the field. I met my officer early that morning and we drove to the field that was to be hunted. I was dropped off and told to walk halfway down the dove field, being mindful of not leaving boot tracks, and set up in a ditch next to a large weeping willow tree. I arrived at the tree and slid into the ditch. Water was standing about six inches deep in the ditch, and the only dry place to stand was on a root from the willow tree. Now all I had to do was wait about five hours for the hunters to arrive to hunt.

After about forty-five minutes, my feet were killing me from standing on the stumps. I would shift right and then left, trying to give each foot a rest and some circulation so they won't go to sleep. I had brought my military Alice pack with snacks, water, ticket book, binoculars, notepad, insect spray, rainsuit in case it rained, radio, sun screen, AA battery fan and anything else I could think of to make my day more comfortable. I can't ever remember a day that I was not over-prepared for work. At about 1100. a pickup truck arrived at the field and parked on the edge of the road. The hunters got out and began scouting the fields for birds. The field was not thick with birds, but it was looking like it could be a very good hunt if the conditions changed some. The hunters began their walk to the back and sides of the field, and one particular hunter decided to put his five-gallon bucket seat next to the willow tree that I was hiding under. I watched him load his shotgun with three shells, sit down on the bucket and begin his wait. The first part of the hunt was hot, with little bird activity. About 1430 some clouds rolled in and the wind picked up some and cooled things off, thank goodness, and the birds started flying a little better. I made notes of what my hunter was wearing as well as the hunter in the middle of the field, about seventy-five yards away. My notes consisted of descriptions of each hunter, what time each hunter shot, how many times they shot, and whether they killed a bird and put it in their bag or killed a bird and did not retrieve it. At the end of the day, if you had detected any violations and confronted the hunter, once you started telling him exactly what he did that day, there was nothing he could argue about.

My hunter started off slow, killing very few birds. He shot a lot, but most of the birds that were too far away. By the way, my hunter also brought his Lab to retrieve his birds for him. That was good for him but not so great for me. A couple of times the Lab poked his nose in the tree limbs and start sniffing me. I had to "shoo" him away several times, but very quietly so as not to get caught by his master. My hunter finally did shoot one bird, and the bird fell in the ditch next to the tree I was standing on. The hunter walked up to the tree and moved the limbs around a few times looking for the bird, but he couldn't find it. He then sent his dog in to retrieve his bird. The dog walked into the ditch and right up to me. I reached down and picked up the bird and handed it to the dog. He put the bird into his mouth and ran out with it when his master called him. "Good boy, good boy," his master said.

After a while the hunter walked back to the pickup trucks by the road to get a snack and a drink. I figured this would be a good time to climb up the bank of the ditch on the opposite side of the field and rest my feet. I sat under the willow limbs to stay concealed. Soon I saw the hunter returning to his gear by the tree to start hunting again. My feet hurt so bad, I decided to stay where I was and keep the willow limbs over me. He hadn't been back for ten minutes when I saw him shoot another bird. This time the bird fell on the side of the ditch that I was on, right next to me. I lay as still as I could and very slowly pulled some more willow limbs over me for concealment. The hunter sent his dog over the ditch to retrieve his bird. "Get him, boy, get him, find the bird, and find the bird." That dog jumped the ditch and came right for me. When he was about six feet away, I tossed the bird into the open where the dog could find him. The dog sniffed around for a while, peed on my tree limbs and saw the bird. He walked over, picked up the bird and continued to walk to me. The dog stuck his head into the limbs I was holding down and started sniffing me. I patted him on the head and he turned and jumped back over the ditch to his master. "Good boy, good boy, you da man." Yes sirree, that was some good dog he had. Two birds shot and I handed them to the dog to take back.

The rest of the day was pretty uneventful, with my hunter killing five birds. When the hunt was over, all of the hunters started walking back to their trucks. I stepped out of the ditch and was walking behind my hunter. He didn't even know that I was behind him until I told him what a great dog he had. He turned and grinned when he saw me. He asked if I wanted to check his birds. "No thanks," I said, and I began reading from my notes how many times he shot and how many birds he killed. I never did tell him about how I helped his dog with the birds. I didn't want to burst his bubble.

November 2001

I was sitting at the house when I got a call from a hunter in Aurora about a man that had just shot a deer near their hunting camp. Members of the club went to the field and saw an old tow truck quickly driving away from the scene. One of the members went out into the field and found a small doe that had just been shot. This was the point at which the hunters called me. I drove to Aurora and turned onto Hunting Camp Road, and after about a two-mile drive I was at the camp. The president of the club met me at the vehicle and said that they had just seen a small blue Nissan pickup truck stop by the field and then take off when they saw members of the club drive to that area again. He stated that I should have passed the vehicle as I was coming up the road, but I had not. I asked the president to take me to the field so I could set up and watch the deer, which he did. He also showed me a place to park my car and watch the field. I dropped off the president, drove back to the field, backed into the "hole" and began my long wait.

Getting bored, I got out of the car, took my chair out of the trunk, and walked to the road. I sat my chair up near the road in a position where I could see traffic going from either way. The night was a little cool and it was a perfect, cloudless night. After a while I was getting bored again and so I decided to walk up and down the road to get some exercise. This "exercise" period lasted about forty minutes, with me having to jump into the ditch a couple of times to avoid being detected by oncoming traffic. At about 2200, I noticed a vehicle coming from the north end of the road and shining a Q-Beam light from the passenger window. The shining lasted only a few seconds and then the vehicle traveled closer to my setup. As it got nearer, it again shined the light out of the passenger window into the field that I was watching, and then turned the light down the path in which I was sitting. When the light struck my car, the vehicle turned the light off and took off down the road at a high rate of speed.

I ran to my car, jumped in and began my pursuit to catch up with the vehicle. By the time my car hit the pavement the vehicle in question was almost out of sight. I stomped onto the accelerator to make up time, but I was getting nowhere fast. I noticed that the vehicle turned to the right onto a dirt road and about fifteen seconds later I made the same turn. I couldn't see a thing. There was dust and dirt everywhere. It was all I could do to see the road. I slowed my pursuit and kept driving. When I got to an intersection I noticed that the vehicle had turned right onto another dirt road. I knew that if

I was going to catch the vehicle, I was going to have to tighten up a little. I pushed my car a little harder, and the dust was really flying now. As I entered a short curve to the left, I also noticed a railroad crossing. Knowing I was almost on the vehicle, I kept the accelerator down and drove over the railroad crossing. It was at this point I realized how Santa Claus must have felt upon first taking off in his sleigh at a slight upward angle and looking up and seeing nothing but stars, because that was all that I could see, except of course a soybean field as a landing strip. All I could think about first was landing in that field. The second thing that came to mind was "OH CRAP!" I turned the wheel to the left, but the steering wheel felt really loose. Tires seem to turn really easily when they are suspended off the ground about four feet.

As my vehicle landed back on the road it went into a left turn, with the rear end sliding to the right. I started to fish tail and found it hard to bring her back under control, but I proceeded with my pursuit. On a straight of way, I started making up time and distance, and I finally got the vehicle stopped. I ran to the truck and told two young boys to get out, move to the front of the truck, and stand in their headlights while I searched the truck for a weapon. The two boys were a little nervous, and they gave me permission. I looked in and under EVERYTHING. I just knew that I had the guys responsible for shooting the deer. After a few minutes of intense searching, I had to give up. I scolded the boys and left to return to my Sig 1. I backed into my setup and threw the parachute over my car and got ready for a long wait.

I walked back out to the road and knew that I had blown my cover. The whole world had to know that I was down there working now. I thought for a moment and finally decided to close up shop for the night. I walked back out into the field and over to where the deer was supposed to be lying, and the deer was gone. I had been setup, BIG TIME. The vehicle that shined was a decoy to draw me out, which it did, and while I was chasing that vehicle another vehicle had come by and picked up the deer. And in all probability it was the same small pickup seen in that area when I first got there. All I could do was laugh. I got to admit it; they knew EXACTLY what they were doing. I told myself that it would never happen again.

April 11, 2003

At about 2330 it was time to go to work. Sergeant Eddie Morton had called that afternoon and asked for some help sitting on eight different baited turkey sites in Craven County. One of my officers, my lieutenant and I were selected to go help out. I worked in Area 2 District 2, and we were going to assist an officer in another area, Area 3 District 2. I drove to a housing community on the Intracoastal Waterway in Carteret County and met with four other officers from Area 3. The officer stationed in that county would be dropping us at each one of the baited sites by boat. He had received reports of the baited sites the past week. These violators were hunting some Weyerhaeuser property without permission and had been entering the property by water, moving inland about a hundred yards and then putting out corn for turkey. If they came the next morning, we would be there waiting for them. We rode in the officer's Tahoe for what seemed like forever down some pretty tough paths to the Intracoastal Waterway, launched our boat and then rode another twenty minutes by water to set up. We had to run blackout to keep from being seen and my lieutenant was a little nervous, to say the least.

He had been involved in a serious boating accident on South Creek in Aurora on July 28, 2002 while he was returning from a night boating detail in Washington. Their Wildlife boat had hit a sailboat that was anchored in the channel of South Creek without anchor lights, and my lieutenant had been thrown from the boat. It took him and another officer a little time to get over it and he was still a little nervous about being on a boat, especially at night without lights. One of the officers asked him why he was working so early in the morning in a boat. He replied that if he had known he was going to be put in a boat, at night, with no lights, he would have stayed home. Everyone laughed and then asked him if he wanted the other officer that was with him to operate the boat. The LT (lieutenant) stated, rather intensely, "HELL NO." Anyway, my LT was the first one to be dropped out, and then me. I had to walk about ten yards in the water and then I found some dry land. I walked another twenty-five yards and then reached some tall pine trees. The turkey bait was supposed to be in the group of trees about seventy-five yards in front of me. The next thing I had to do was to find a spot to watch for the hunter coming in that morning and make sure I wasn't in the line of fire.

I found three tall pine trees pretty close together and began to make camp. The ground was damp, so I laid a heavy survival blanket down and piled my gear on top on that. Then I stretched some parachute cord about two feet off the ground from one tree, wound it around the second, and tied it tight to the third tree. Then I laid a mosquito net over the parachute cord and secured one end of the net to the ground with a tent spike. I inflated a military air mattress that I just happened to have, and then laid a Gore-Tex bivy on top of the mattress. It was supposed to get down to about 45 degrees that night, and lying on the damp ground next to the water would make it even colder. I crawled into my bivy and decided that I would rest my eyes until daylight. It was now 0300 in the morning. I closed my eyes for just a moment and then opened them to find it was 0600 in the morning. The sun was starting to come up, and I didn't know if the man I was supposed to be waiting for had come or not. I was kind of scared to move for fear that he might think that I was a turkey and shoot at me. I lay there for a little while and didn't hear anything. That was good news. If a man was turkey hunting, he would be trying to call one in, and that wasn't happening. I decided to give him a little more time before I stood up to stretch.

After about thirty more minutes, I was convinced that no one was hunting at the bait pile that I was watching. It was a little cold, so I decided to make some coffee and heat up some breakfast with a stove that I always kept with me. I made a cup of vanilla nut coffee, lit up a cigar and watched the sun come up over the water. Now this, I thought, is what I call working. As the sun reflected off the water and into the woods where I was sitting, I could hear ducks taking off out of the creek to the right of me and flying past my setup. You could hear the sound of air moving through their wings, making a sort of swooshing sound as they went by me. That was the only sound you could hear that time of the morning. I watched this sight until about 0930. That was when I heard a boat coming up the creek, and saw that it was my ride back out. I packed up my gear, got into the boat and shoved off. As we were entering the big water, an old tri-hull boat with two guys dressed in camo was heading to the creek we had just left. They saw us, stopped and began talking to each other. After a while they turned their boat and headed back the way they had come. We looked at each other and then at the officer in charge. He said that they were the guys we were waiting for. We figured we wouldn't have to worry about that bait site for a while.

Deer Decoy
December 1988

As all wildlife officers probably do and I did as a young wildlife officer, I loved to read stories about deer poaching and the methods used to catch these poachers. Sometime in the mid-1980's wildlife officers from other states began using robotic deer. In the early years of robotic deer, they were made from taxidermy deer forms used when mounting a full-sized deer. These deer were made from a condensed foam in the shape of a deer with a ⅜-inch threaded rod inserted into each of the four legs. The head of the foam deer was cut off and model airplane servos were placed into the neck and in the deer's butt area to get movement from the deer. The servo in the neck would allow the deer's head to look left and right, and the butt servo would allow the tail to wag. A deerskin was then mounted over the form, with cuts made for the head and tail areas to move. I was lucky enough to be sent to a school to learn how to make these deer while in District 3, which included Warren County and again in District 2, which included my duty station in Pitt County.

A GAME WARDEN'S ADVENTURE

It took a lot of coaxing and research for our Raleigh office supervisors to approve the purchase and use of decoys but when they did, the officer in the field had a great tool for catching road hunters, trespassers, and night time deer hunting poachers. But before the authorization to use these decoys, many officers came up with their own methods of catching these poachers. My method was simple — one tobacco stick about four feet tall with a short piece, approximately four inches long, nailed to the top in the shape of a cross. I would then use Bright Eyes, or tacks that would reflect a flashlight, placed on the short piece to simulate that eyes of a deer. With the tall tobacco stick stuck in the ground just inside the wood line in the back of a field, poachers shining a spotlight looking for deer would think there was a deer standing just in the wood line. To make it look even more real, I made the same setup, but only about two feet tall, to simulate a fawn deer or deer laying on the ground. I was now ready. There really was no WRC policy prohibiting this, because no one talked about these things except to their VERY good friends.

The next night I decided to try out my "decoys" on a firelighting detail near Churchill in northern Warren County. I would be setting up and hiding my car behind an old house that was partially fallen in on Hub Quarter Road, just a few hundred yards north of Fleming Mill Road. It was a perfect place to work. The field was directly across the road from my hiding place. I parked behind the house and took my "decoy" with me to the field. I walked down the tree line on the left side of the field so I could hide if cars approached from either direction and made my way to the back right corner of the field. I stuck the two "decoys" in the dirt and ran back to my patrol vehicle and began my wait. It was cold, with a slight frost on the ground, and a half moon was lighting the roadway. Just a few days before, I was celebrating Christmas, and now I was working alone. It was a still and quiet night — just the type of night that I loved while working firelighting. It was definitely more dangerous than daytime work, and I don't know how to explain it, but I was never really scared to work by myself.

I had been sitting for about two hours when I noticed an old station wagon approach the field and slow down. It came to a stop, and moments later a light came from the driver's window, shining across the top of the station wagon into the field and onto my "deer." I put my hand on the ignition key and got ready. This was the moment when your heart starts racing and you're mouthing the words, "Shoot it, shoot it." You're waiting to hear the report of a rifle echo on a cold night. You could hear that shot forever, and suddenly I did hear it echoing through the quiet night. I started the car and drove as fast as I could to the station wagon as it was starting to pull away. I stopped the station wagon about a quarter of a mile down the road. I approached the driver side, shining my flashlight at the driver, as I saw no passenger. I asked him to step out of the station wagon and recognized him right away. I looked in the back seat floorboard and saw a pump shotgun as well.

Now this guy was the son of some friends of mine who lived at Lake Gaston Estates. I said. "What in the hell are you doing?' He stated, "Nothing." I told him what I saw and issued a citation instead of arresting him. The next day I drove to his parents' house to talk to them, since I knew they would have a lot of questions. I learned from talking to them that there was another man involved who was the passenger. The passenger had shot from his window as the driver held the light. When I started my car I could not hear the passenger door of the station wagon shut as the passenger got out to pick up his "deer." I found out the name of the passenger and paid him a visit to issue him a citation as well. Normally we arrest for all night deer hunting violations, but because I did not feel he would skip out of his court date, I issued the citation.

October 1995

Before Gordon Hobbs came to Greene County I had another officer stationed there. His name was Ken Bell. Ken lived in a small house just south and east of Snow Hill. One evening Ken received a call from a landowner saying that some Latino people staying in a migrant house on the next farm over from his, across the line in Pitt County, were crossing over to his property in the afternoons and shooting deer on his property. Milton Jones, a Pitt County officer, stopped by the house and picked me up and we headed over to meet Ken. Ken told us about his report and said that he wanted to use the deer decoy to try and catch these guys. We got everything loaded up in the truck and it was decided that I would be the guy on the ground working the decoy remote control. We drove over to the farm of the complainant. Ken knew a back way into the farm where he could hide his truck. We parked and walked over to where we could see the migrant house and determine where to set up the decoy.

The migrant house was pretty large and was sitting on a hill in the middle of a field. When a person walked out of that house, he had about a seventy-five yard walk down a straight path in an open field, and then the path turned to the left and went down the hill to a small tractor bridge used for crossing into the next field. Once you crossed the bridge, you were in the complainant's field. Approximately thirty yards from the bridge was a tobacco barn with a short field about a hundred yards square. It was decided that I would set the deer up in the back corner of the field and then move back to the tobacco barn to hide. This was a great spot to hide, because it also had another door directly across from the entrance that I could use to watch the migrant house and anyone coming or going. I looked down the field and could see that the decoy was working as I moved one of the control handles on the remote. I was ready. I did forget to mention that I brought my Browning BPS 12-gauge shotgun with me, just in case. I found a place to sit inside the barn and began watching the migrant house. We had gotten to the field at about 1500, so the wait would not be long until sunset.

At about 1700, I noticed some movement on the outside of the house. I saw one male leave the house, walk a short distance in my direction and then turn around and go back to the house. A short time later I notice a woman and two small children leave the house, walking my way down the path. When they had gotten about fifty yards from the house, a male walked out of the door and evidently told the female to stop, because she did. He was carrying some type of long gun with him. When he reached her they began walking down the hill toward the bridge. I called Ken and Milton and told them to get ready, that we had company. The child was throwing rocks as the man and woman walked together, talking. They crossed the bridge and walked to within ten feet of the barn I was in. As they reached the field the man saw the decoy and motioned for the woman to stop. It was then that I noticed that the rifle was a 22-caliber semi-automatic.

The man slowly crouched on the ground, propped his left arm on his knee and took careful aim. I moved the head slightly with my remote control and wagged the tail. He fired four shots and then stopped. He looked over his scope at the decoy and went back into his shooting position. This time he fired five rounds. Not knowing if his scope was off or not, he said something to the female, stood up and took careful aim again. I did not want to exit the barn until it was safe, so I let him shoot some more. This time he fired to lock back (until he was empty and the bolt was locked back). He couldn't believe what he was seeing. He put the rifle stock on the ground and pulled the magazine tube out of the gun to reload. It was my time to move. I stepped out of the barn and racked my pump shotgun, although not really necessary, and pointed the muzzle in the air. They were stunned. I held the shotgun with my left hand and said something like "Policia" and motioned for the male to lay the rifle on the ground. I walked up and moved the rifle from the ground and waited about thirty seconds for Ken and Milton to show up. Now, Milton has a way of getting a point across where you really can understand what he is saying, even if you don't know the language. He is not condescending and is as polite as the situation allows. This particular time, he wasn't having a lot of luck.

He asked the man if he knew what he had done and if he knew it was against the law, but the man shook his head. After a few more of "no comprendes", Milton asked him, "Well, do you understand judge?" This time the answer was "si." Milton then told the man that he was going to get to see the judge. Ken motioned for the woman to take the children back to the house and she left. Milton handcuffed the man, and we all loaded up into the truck heading to the Pitt County Detention Center to see the "judge" or more correctly, the magistrate. Once there, the man was taken before the magistrate and I waited outside with the truck. After a few minutes Milton came out and said, "Well Sarg, Juan now understands four new English words – "judge" and "five hundred dollars." We do what we can when we can to bridge cultural differences.

A GAME WARDEN'S ADVENTURE

November 1998

One day one of my officers in Pitt County needed assistance in working the deer decoy on the Stokestown-St. Johns Road in southern Pitt County. I had many responsibilities as Sergeant, and one of those was to work with any of my officers when they needed help. This was especially true working the deer decoy. It was definitely a two-man detail. One officer was dropped out on the field that we needed to work and the other officer drove the chase vehicle, hidden just down the road a little ways. You really had to be quick to get your field pack – full-sized deer decoy with removable head and remote control — out of the vehicle and into a hiding spot next to the field when dropped out of the patrol vehicle. Once you were out of the vehicle, the driver would speed away to his "Sig 1," or area of assignment. On this detail, I was to work the remote control decoy. I was dropped off on the road, got everything out of the vehicle, jumped across the ditch and ran for some weeds, approximately three feet tall, in the field.

Once there, I lay on the ground very still, listening for any cars or trucks moving on the road. The officer in the car would also listen and radio me if he heard any vehicles moving my way. Lying in the weeds I didn't hear anything, so I put my field pack on my back and picked up the deer and remote and ran toward the corner of some woods next to the field. After running only about fifty yards, I heard a truck coming and so I dove on the ground and got as small as I could. After the truck passed by the field,

I again picked up the deer and started to run to the woods. Again I heard a vehicle coming my way after only another thirty to forty yards, and again I dove to the ground. I was starting to get pretty good at this. I wasn't nearly as tired as I thought I would be. It felt like I was playing army like when I was a kid – running and diving in the dirt. Anyway, I listened hard again and heard nothing, so I got up a third time and ran for all I was worth. I could hear a vehicle coming my way but with no more weeds to dive into, I just had to run hard and hope he didn't see me. As I got closer to the wood line I could hear the vehicle passing the field and I knew that he probably hadn't seen me because of how fast he was traveling. He wasn't out looking for deer in a field; he wanted to go home. I dove into the woods as he passed by and caught my breath. I sat for a minute and took a sip of water.

Now I had to get the deer out into the field a little ways and about seventy-five yards along the wood line from me. I walked inside the wood line to the spot I wanted and stepped out to set the deer up. After putting the head on and facing it toward the road, I checked the remote to make sure the deer was operational. It was, and I ran back to corner of the woods and the field to set up behind a tree. It was a cool, quiet, clear fall day with the sun just beginning to set. I loved this time of the day. Suddenly I heard some movement behind me. I turned and saw a hunter sitting in a tree stand with his blaze orange cap on, which wasn't on before, and his rifle lying across his knees. He said, "This ought to be fun, can I watch?" I was stunned and said, "Sure, come on down." While he was on his way down the tree, I called Milton and told him to head this way. There was a path beside the field where he could hide his vehicle. I then apologized to the hunter (about ten times) for messing his hunt up for that day. He told me not to worry about it. He was one of the people who had called the Wildlife Commission to get us to work a decoy in that spot. My officer got there with his car and we put the parachute over it. We worked the decoy for about an hour, with no luck catching a poacher, before we packed up.

A couple of days later, Milton wanted to work the decoy again in the same general area as our last detail. That day we were going to a field near Helen's Cross Roads. This field wasn't huge, but it had a lot going for it. The field extended to a small strip of woods next to a creek that crossed the road, and best of all there was an old barn sitting about 200 yards off the road and in the middle of the field. I thought we would park the car behind the barn and put the deer up about 100 yards off the road, right next to the tree line. Milton, however, had different plans. There was a drainage ditch running at an angle from the road, across the field and back into the woods, which was now about 250 yards from the road. His great suggestion was to set the decoy in the ditch, with only the head and antlers showing. I questioned his theory about the set up and all he said was, "Just watch." We got the decoy up and hid behind the barn. We tested the head movement, which worked great. I told him there was no need to test the tail because you couldn't even see the darn thing. Oh well, I thought, we'll see.

We hadn't been there more than an hour when we heard a truck moving on the road, approaching the field. It was traveling west, toward the creek, and it would pass the entire length of the field, with plenty of time to see the decoy, if we had put it where I wanted to. The truck did not attempt to slow down until it completely passed the field and was hidden from us. We heard the roar of the tires slow down, and eventually we heard nothing. We were both watching the edge of the field and the road with our binoculars when we spotted a young man tiptoeing back to the field with a rifle in his hand with another young man close behind him. They slowly walked to where they could see the deer, stopped and knelt down in the middle of the road. The shooter brought his scoped rifle up to his shoulder and took his time. You could hear Milton and me both whispering, "Shoot, shoot." All of a sudden, there was a loud crack from his rifle. He stopped shooting and looked over the top of his scope at the decoy. I slowly moved the head with the remote control, and he fired two more times. Milton jumped in the patrol car and flew out of the field and down to the truck. When they saw him coming, both boys started walking back to the truck really quickly. I saw the blue light come on and Milton get out of the car.

A short time later, Milton called me and said the boys wanted to know if they hit the deer. I told him to stand by and I would bring it to them. I walked to the ditch and retrieved the decoy and walked out to the field to the road. Just before I jumped the ditch to the road, I removed the decoy head and lay in some weeds. I really didn't want these two guys to know exactly what our decoy looked like so they couldn't spread the word around town. I carried the decoy to the back of the patrol car and told the boys to come on over. Because the deer was already shot full of holes, you couldn't see the fresh bullet holes just by looking at it, but if you lay the deer on the exit wound side and tapped the side of the deer on the road, fresh foam would fall out of the holes, identifying your bullet holes. Before I did this, I asked the shooter where his point of aim was on the deer. He stated just behind the front shoulder, in the chest. I tapped the deer on the road surface and the foam dust revealed the bullet holes. I told him he was shooting about six inches high and to the right some. He just chuckled and said he needed to sight his rifle in a little better. The charges for the two boys were hunting on the road and not wearing blaze orange.

November 1998

One afternoon I got a call from my officer in Greene County for help with a report that he had received. I met with Gordon Hobbs at his home and we drove to the location of his "hunting from the road" report. On the way over he told me that we would be looking for an older model Mustang coupe, dark in color and driven by a Latino male living at the end of a dead end dirt road. Everything sounded like the usual stuff that we worked, except when he told me the driver of the

Mustang had a SKS 7.62x39 in the back glass on the Mustang. He was reported to be shooting deer from his vehicle in the surrounding area of a farmhouse housing several Latino families working for local farmers. He would then bring the meat back to be eaten by everyone staying in the house. Most of the time, this was the case with Latinos finding work and then staying in the area. During the summer months we got a lot of reports of this kind of activity. Anyway, we got close to the road we wanted to work but parked away from that road until we had everything ready to go. I had my usual gear — backpack with camo tarp, mosquito netting, water, snacks, flashlight, bug spray, binoculars and radio. I got the decoy ready to go and Gordon drove down the dirt road about a quarter mile and stopped. He showed me the spot he wanted the deer placed and showed me where I could hide.

I jumped out of the truck and threw all of my gear in a weeded ditch, and then Gordon left the area. I listened for movement for about five minutes but heard nothing. I carried all of my gear into the woods and then returned for the decoy. I sat for about ten more minutes to listen for cars moving or anyone walking down the road. Feeling confident that it was clear, I carried the decoy across the dirt road and up a ditch incline of about ten feet but still on the right of the road. I set up the decoy and made sure that everything was working properly. I then ran back across the road and into the woods about twenty yards. It was November, and although there were some leaves still on the trees most had fallen, giving me a good view of the road plus good concealment. I lay my tarp out to sit on, put my gear on the tarp and then lay down under the mosquito netting for camo. About five minutes later, Gordon called me to check communications and I responded that all was well. I did not have a vehicle to drive by my setup for about one and a half hours. Gordon then called me and told me that a car was turning off of the main road and heading my way.

I could hear the rocks popping as the tires ran over them and knew that it was traveling slowly and getting closer. As the car got to where the decoy was set up, the brake lights came on and the car stopped about twenty yards from the decoy. The windows of the car were down and I could hear a man and woman talking, but I could not understand a thing that they were saying. I whispered into the radio and told Gordon that they had stopped by the decoy and to get ready. The driver's door began to open very slowly and a male slipped from the car and got into a crouched position behind the front left tire. The driver began to slowly walk down the road past the decoy in a crouched position. I used the remote and turned the decoy's head to look at the driver. He immediately stopped, still in the crouched position and not moving a muscle. I then noticed that a woman had also exited the car and was slowly climbing the embankment in the direction of the deer. I turned the decoy's head to look directly at her and she froze. As she was crouching very still, the man, again, began to move down the road. I turned the head back to him and he again froze. When he stopped, the woman began to move again. The decoy looked back at her and, you're right, she froze.

I was trying real hard not to laugh as I watched these two, and I whispered into the radio to Gordon to just sit tight for a while. The movement from the man and woman continued back and forth until they were each about six to seven feet on either side from the deer. All of a sudden both the man and woman lunged for the decoy, grabbing the small six-point rack. I called Gordon and told him to come on to the decoy ASAP. Just as I looked up, I could see both the man and woman holding the fake head in their hands and rambling on about something. Gordon pulled up and I walked out of the woods to meet him. I walked up the incline and took the decoy head from them and motioned for the two to come down to the patrol vehicle where I asked for their ID's. They were both laughing, as were we, and we told them what they were doing was illegal and that they had to leave the area. As they were heading back to their car, we heard another vehicle approaching us. We had nowhere to go, and so just stood there watching headlights getting closer. Soon we saw a dark, older model Mustang with one person in the car. It slowed as it approached us but did not stop, and then it drove on by us. As it went by us, we noticed an SKS rifle laying in the back glass.

My officer in Pitt County had received a report of someone shooting deer very early in the morning on

Leary Mills Road in lower Pitt County. He called and asked me if I wanted to work the deer decoy with him in that area, and I told him I was ready to go. The report pointed to a man who was using a small pickup truck to deliver the newspaper to residents in that area. I rode with Milton to the area and we found a nice straight of way only about a quarter mile off of Highway 102 and Leary Mills Road. This was a great spot to work because there was a dirt path off the Leary Mills Road right in the middle of the strait of way. We got to the area about 0330 – 0400 and parked on the dirt path. I got the deer decoy and carried it to the road. Making sure no one was coming, I ran out to the road and set the deer on the side of the road next to the southbound lane. Now all we had to do was wait.

I found a spot on the opposite side of the road from the deer, where I could still see the deer to work the head and tail with my remote control. There were some thick bushes where I could hide if a vehicle came by. About 0530 we heard a truck turn south off of Highway 102, and soon I could see the headlights coming straight toward me. I got into my hiding spot and waited for the truck to get closer. When the truck was about seventy-five yards out I turned the decoy's head to look straight at the vehicle. The glow tacks that I had mounted in the decoy's eyes lit up like two flashlights. The vehicle, a small pickup, slowed and turned its headlights to the right some to focus fully on the decoy. The truck stopped, and I heard the driver's side door open very slowly. I whispered into my radio to Milton to get ready, the driver was going to shoot. Everything was quiet for about 15 seconds, which is a long time waiting for someone to shoot.

Suddenly fire came from the barrel of his gun, and the report of the gun echoed through the cold early morning. I began yelling, "State wildlife officer! Step from the truck and put your gun on the ground!" You could tell that he thought about it, but just briefly. I heard Milton's patrol vehicle coming my way just as the pickup took off. I shined my light in the driver's eyes as he came by me to see what he looked like, and then Milton's vehicle came out of the path like a bolt of lightning. I jumped out of the way and watched as the two vehicles went out of sight, Milton's siren screaming in the night. I could hear the siren for about five minutes, and then it was dead quiet — just me and my decoy, alone, standing by the edge of the road. I took the decoy down so no one else would come by and shoot it, laid it by the dirt path and sat down by the edge of the road. It was at this time I remembered something very important. I had a thermos of coffee in my backpack, along with a Cohiba cigar.

For about thirty minutes I didn't hear anything from Milton, and then the radio came to life. He called and said that he had the vehicle stopped on Highway 102 west of me and that his vehicle was out of commission. It seems while he was chasing the pickup through a vehicle junkyard his back right tire had been cut. He said he noticed his vehicle acting a little squirrelly when they came to a paved road again but just kept the gas pedal down. Then, all of a sudden, the pickup just pulled over to the side of the road, and the driver just gave up. It was a good thing. Milton had run the tire off of the rim. He contacted the Pitt County Sheriff's Department, and before long a deputy was taking Milton and his prisoner to the Magistrate's Office and the other deputy came to pick me up. I hid the decoy in the woods so Milton and I could get it later while we came back to get his patrol vehicle.

It was the opening day of deer season in Warren County, and not being able to find another officer to work with me, I decided to work by myself – setting up the deer decoy on Major Rob Alston Road located beside the Lickskillet Game Lands at the southernmost location of Warren County. It was a Monday morning. I knew the area extremely well, as I had a very good friend that lived next to the Game Lands, and we hunted on his property there. I had gotten to my setup at about 0300 in the morning, backed my Bronco into a grown-over path and put the parachute over the vehicle. The field I wanted to work was across the road from me and belonged to my buddy. I got the decoy out of my Bronco and turned on the controls to make sure it worked by turning the head and tail motors. It looked good, so I checked for traffic and ran across the road. I worked my way down the right hand side of the field, and when I had gotten about seventy-five yards in the field, I ran to the center of the field and set the decoy up. I ran back to the wood line and listened for any vehicles moving before I made my way to the Bronco. I then pulled out my chair and sat by the Bronco waiting for a poacher to come by.

All was quiet until about 0530. I started to hear rocks on the dirt road popping from the weight of the vehicle, and soon I noticed a full-size pickup come by my setup very slowly. I threw the chair into the bushes and got in the driver's seat of the Bronco. The pickup stopped in front of the field with my decoy, and my heartbeat started to pick up. I love hearing a rifle shot when the night is still. Suddenly I saw a flash of light, and I started my Bronco. Then it dawned on me that I did not hear a shot, so I cut the motor off. Again I saw a flash of light but heard no shot. I eased to the dirt road and saw two men standing beside their truck taking pictures of my deer. What tha?? Not wanting these two guys to scare away anyone wanting to shoot a deer illegally, I started the Bronco and drove blackout to the truck in the road. I turned on my headlights and immediately saw a rifle hanging in the back glass in a gun rack.

I got out of my Bronco and walked to the men, who seemed to be very excited. "How are you guys doing this morning" I asked. "Sir, that deer in the field is not acting right. I think it's been hit by a car. It just stands there looking at us and every now and then barely moves its head." I'm thinking, OK, at least they're not trying to shoot my deer. I asked if the men hunted with any of the clubs in Warren County and they stated that they did. They were coming in from Raleigh, about sixty miles south of us, to hunt the date with their club members. One of the guys said, "It might be sick." I took my rechargeable Maglite out and shined it on the deer. "Look, it's not even moving the least little bit," one man said. I said, "Let me try something. Sir, you hold my Maglite on the deer and I'll be right back." At that point I walked back to the Bronco, retrieved my remote control and walked back to the men. I stood close enough to the man holding my flashlight that my elbow was touching his elbow. I pulled the antenna on the remote up and turned it on. With my right hand I began working the remote to make the deer head move just slightly.

"LOOK, LOOK. He's trying to move his head!" one man said. I then used the remote to turn his head as far to the right as it would go and then back to facing us. The two men just kept repeating, "He's sick or he's been hit by a car." I turned to the men, turned the remote off and put the antenna down. I said, "Guys, I think you're right. Let's leave the area, and maybe he'll run back into the woods." Both men turned to go to their truck. I walked back with them and asked to see their rifle that was hanging up to see if it was loaded. Now up to this point, no one had shined a light looking for deer, whether handheld or by using the headlights, and it was DANG obvious that no one was trying to poach a deer. I explained the night deer hunting element to them, and then both men left. Oh brother. It was going to be one of those deer seasons.

A GAME WARDEN'S ADVENTURE

November 8, 1999

Our deer decoys worked great as long as the violator didn't shoot a round through the neck and hit the motor. It he did, it usually left a hole about the size of your hand on the exit wound side of the neck. Not good. It would usually take a half of can of Bondo to fill the hole. On this particular detail, about sixteen officers met in Kenansville to pair up. We normally worked in pairs so we would have a chase car and a man on foot to work the remote. I was paired up with one of my men, Tony Cox, and was given a location to work. It happened to be in my work area in Greene County along the Lenoir/Greene County line. We found the road we were told to work and a nice long straight-of-way with a sharp curve to the left at the end of the road. Tony dropped me out with the deer at about 1700 and I ran along the edge of the field and along the wood line to a spot about a hundred fifty yards off the road. It was a perfect spot to catch a road hunter. I set the deer up and then ran back to the other side of the road to wait. It wasn't long before our first vehicle came down the road, slowed down and stopped right in front of the deer.

I called Tony and told him to get ready, that we had a shooter. The truck pulled off the road and onto the grass with the driver side of the vehicle facing toward the deer. After a second or two, I saw the driver roll the window down, and then I saw the muzzle end of a rifle slowly inching its way out of the window. The movement of the rifle stopped, and then I saw and heard the shot come from the rifle. I called Tony and told him to come on. I also yelled to the driver, "State Wildlife Officer! Turn the vehicle's motor off and step out of the truck. Lay the weapon on the ground!" You could see the driver shaking his head from within the truck cab, and he did as he was told. I waited until Tony arrived before I stepped from the protection of my setup behind a tree in the woods and then walked to the truck. The first thing he said to me was, "How much is this going to cost?" We answered the man's questions, cited him, seized his weapon for court and sent him on his way. Another dissatisfied violator.

We figured we were having so much fun, why leave the area? We did, however, decide to move our location down the road a few hundred yards to another long straight section of the road for our next mission. The time was about 1845 hours. This time instead of the wood line, I decided to set the deer out on the state road right-of-way, just on the ditch bank. That way when a car approached from either direction, I could turn his head and look at the vehicle approaching. I forgot to mention that I had put a tack with reflective tape near each eye so the light would reflect back to the vehicle, making it look even more real. Tony dropped me out on the straight-of-way at my "Sig 1." There wasn't much cover there, only soybean fields on either side, so finding a place to hide would be tough. We normally liked to place ourselves on the opposite side of the road from the side where the deer was set up, for safety reasons. That is, I didn't want to get shot. I set the deer up and moved to the other side of the road and out into the bean field about 10 yards. I laid my poncho on the ground in the beans and settled in for the wait. It didn't take long.

After only about a ten-minute wait, I heard the sound of truck tires coming down the road. I lay down in the beans as flat as I could, hoping the headlights wouldn't hit me and give my position away. I watched as the headlights from the truck swept around a short curve in the road and then hit the decoy. I immediately saw brake lights from the rear of the truck and it slowed down, turning just slightly to the right putting the full force of the headlights on the deer. Then it stopped. I called Tony and told him to get ready, that I thought that we had a "good one". The term "good one" referred to anyone that we thought looked the part of a violator. The truck just sat there for about thirty seconds, which is a long time doing something like this. I told Tony, again, to stand by and get ready, that the truck was only about twenty steps from me. I sat watching and then heard the sound of door hinges creaking open very slowly. I saw the outline of a man step from the truck and start, VERY slowly, towards the deer. As his legs moved between the headlights and my position, his whole body became silhouetted against the headlights. I looked closer and noticed a long object in his hands. I called Tony and told him that the man had a gun and was trying to get closer to the deer.

As I continued to watch, I saw the man raise the object to his right shoulder and then above his head. I then realized that the man had a long club and was attempting to get close to the deer so he could beat it to death. The man continued VERY slowly, one step methodically placed in front of the other and each time pausing, just a second or two, before repeating his movement. Each time the man took a step, I would move some portion of either the head or the tail on the decoy. Each time he saw the movement, he froze in his tracks. As I watched the man, I could also hear a vehicle approaching from the opposite direction, traveling toward the man in the middle of the road. As the vehicle came around the corner, the man hurriedly turned around, attempting to hide the club, and started walking back to the truck. As the vehicle passed, the man turned around and started his procedure over again, inching his way back in the direction of the deer, one step in front of the other. I was amazed, and I was also trying very hard not to laugh out loud. I covered my mouth and pointed my head toward the ground. I called back to Tony and told him what was happening, that we had us a real hunter out here trying to kill a deer with an ax handle.

Once again, as the man inched his way to the deer, I again heard a vehicle approaching him from the same direction as the last vehicle. This time I watched the man turn and run toward me and the bean field. He jumped the ditch and lay down in the field about ten steps from me. He lay very still as the vehicle passed and then stood to his feet and attempted to inch his way to the deer, but this time from another direction. With each step, I would move the head just slightly and this movement would make the man stop. As the man crossed the ditch, I decided that enough was enough. He was about ten steps from the deer when I called out, "Hey, what are you doing with my deer?" He replied, "Who's there?" I said, "It doesn't matter who it is. That's my deer." The man replied with some dejection in his voice, "Oh, okay," and he started for his truck. About fifteen feet from the truck he stopped, turned in my direction and said "Do you have a gun to kill it with?" I replied, "Yeah." He said "Okay," and started, again, for the truck. Just as be reached the truck he turned and said, "Why don't you come over here and you can shoot him in the headlights of my truck?" I replied, "You'd better get out of here, NOW!" That was all the coaxing he needed. He jumped in the truck and sped away.

To this day, that man doesn't know that he was lying in a field with, and talking to, a game warden.

I started thinking to myself that this was a good spot to work, when lo and behold I could hear another car heading my way. I lay in the soybeans and waited. I watched as the vehicle headlights swept around the curve and onto the deer decoy. The vehicle didn't immediately stop, but slowed and went past the deer about 100 yards, stopped in the road and turned around. I called Tony Cox on the radio and told him to get ready, that I thought that we had a shooter. The vehicle started to the deer, and about fifty yards out he slowly turned his headlights to light the deer up. I heard the driver's door ease open and watched a figure exited the vehicle. I then heard this voice very softly say, "Hey boy. Are you okay?

Here, boy. I'm not going to hurt you. Come here." I then decided to have some more fun. Each time he would say something, I would turn the head just slightly with the remote control.

He couldn't stand it. The man got back into the car and eased the vehicle up to within about twenty feet of the deer. I could still hear him through the driver's window, talking to the deer from inside the car. I decided that I would ask the man to move on because we were working in the area, but as I started toward the deer, the car turned slightly to the left and moved back on the paved portion of the road and proceeded to leave the area. I watched as the car drove off. When he was about a thousand yards away, he pulled into a driveway. After about five minutes, I saw the car returning to the deer. Again he got to within about twenty feet of the deer, but this time I heard a female voice say, "Aw, he's so cute. Are you okay, boy? Are you okay? Come here?" This continued for about five minutes before they decided to leave and go back to the house. I'm thinking, "How many people is he going to bring down here?" I decided to take the deer down, and I ran across the road to the deer. I picked it up just as the car started to return. I ran to the edge of the bean field and lay down on the ground next to the deer. The vehicle stopped, and three people got out and started looking for the deer. After no success, they got back into the vehicle and drove off. I figured that we had outstayed our welcome at this spot, and I called Tony to come get me.

November 16, 1999

I met with Marshall Myers in Washington at the patrol station, and he wanted to work the decoy on the Jackson Swamp Road near Bath. I put all of my gear into his truck, and we were off. We got to the setup about 1645 and set up the decoy. About a half dozen cars and trucks passed by, but none of them took the bait. At about 1715, a white extended cab 4X4 truck drove by and looked down the path where the decoy was set up. This land was registered property, and hunting was restricted without an entry permit. He then turned his truck around and came back to the path, with the driver's side window on the same side as the path. I was at the edge of some woods next to the path, lying down on my poncho. I watched as the barrel of his rifle slid very slowly out of his window. After about one minute, he fired with 300 Weathersby Magnum. I shouted for him to quit shooting, put the gun down, turn the motor of the truck off and step out.

After doing what I had asked, he started shaking his head and said, rather loudly, "That's it. I quit, I quit. I'm not hunting any more this year, I've had enough. Every time I go hunting I get a ticket." He was issued citations for hunting with the aid of a motor vehicle, a registered property violation and not having registered a deer he had killed a week earlier. When asked about the deer, he just said that he hadn't had time to call in for a registration number. I later found out why he had said what he did about not hunting anymore this year. Earlier in the season Marshall had issued him two citations for not validating his big game tags after having killed two deer. I think that I would quit hunting myself after five citations in a two-month period.

December 1999

Working the decoy, although a lot of fun, was also very dangerous. One particular afternoon I met with Gordon Hobbs in Greene County and he decided that he wanted to work the northwest corner of the county near Stantonsburg. Gordon drove to the spot he wanted to work and dropped me out with the decoy. I hid close to the road until Gordon was out of sight. I did this because, before I ran across the road or made any movement, I wanted to survey my surroundings looking for blaze orange, (which might would indicate hunters in a tree stand) and also to listen for vehicles moving. I had to have time to run the decoy out into the field, set it up and then return to my setup before getting caught. On this particular day, the field we were working was a cut hay field, and there were large rolls of hay scattered throughout the field. This was good because it gave me places to hide if I heard a car moving toward my location. I determined that all was quiet, so I sprinted across the road and into the field. I had picked out a spot where I wanted to place the deer and when I was about halfway there, I stopped running, knelt behind a hay bale and listened for any sounds again. I usually listened for five to ten minutes. All was quiet, so

I sprinted to a point about a hundred twenty-five yards from the road to the wood line and set up the deer. Since the deer was brown and tan, I liked to place it in front of a green brushy area next to the woods so that he would stand out more to my hunters. I also liked to place the deer where the setting sun would shine on him until the last possible daylight. This gave us the maximum time to work the field.

Once the deer was set up, I tested the remote control and found the head and tail moving like I wanted. I then ran back across the field to a hay bale next to the road to listen for traffic. Hearing none, I ran across the road where I was first let out, spread out my poncho, poured a cup of coffee and began my wait. The deer looked good out in the field and was directly in front of my setup. The temperature was about forty-five to fifty degrees, so my coffee hit the spot. I waited for about an hour and a half and heard and saw nothing. Just as the sun was setting, I called Gordon (Something is missing here) the road and ran from hay bale to hay bale, stopping every once and a while to listen for sounds.

I made it to the deer, reached under its belly and turned the servo receiver switch off, picked it up and ran back to a hay bale to call Gordon. When all had settled down, I called Gordon and he told me that he was watching a hunter in a field near his setup and he would come get me at dark. I agreed, and not wanting to waste the last fifteen minutes of shooting time, set the deer out once again. This time, though, I stayed behind the hay bale on the same side of the road as the deer, because it was too far to run back to the road and then back out to the deer again. The deer had not been set up for more than five minutes, and it was only about thirty steps from me, when I heard a shot.

There were no vehicles on the road and I was not sure where the shot came from, so I hit the dirt and squeezed as tight as possible next to the hay bale. I was looking toward the woods when I saw a hunter about seventy-five yards from me, without blaze orange, sighting in to make his second shot. I hollered, "State Wildlife Officer. Put weapon on the ground and put your hands in the air!" He appeared to be pretty startled, but he did what he was told. I then called Gordon and told him to come on while I shined my flashlight on the hunter and told him to start walking my way. When Gordon got there, he stopped his truck on the road and walked into the field where we were standing. He asked the hunter for his written permission to be hunting on registered land. He said he was from out of the county, was a schoolteacher and didn't have written permission. Gordon asked him what he was doing there if he had no permission to hunt.

He stated that his buddy from Raleigh hunted in this area, and he thought he would come up to try and find a place to hunt. I asked him if he had seen me enter the field with the decoy deer, and he said that he had not seen me at any time. He told me that he didn't see the deer until he was about thirty yards into the field from the wood line, because it was getting so dark. The scary thing was, the deer was directly in between me and the hunter when my setup was across the road. Had he seen the deer from his stand inside the woods, he would have been shooting directly toward me. When I had moved from the other side of the road from my setup into the field to retrieve the decoy deer, I was then on the same side of the road as the hunter and behind a hay bale, in plain view to him. I was only thirty steps from the decoy deer and only seventy-five steps from where he shot the first time. He was so focused on the deer that he never saw me.

November 25, 1999

It was Thanksgiving Day. I had to meet Tony Cox at 0530 to work a deer decoy detail just north of Washington, NC. He chose the spot, and we drove to the J & W Dismal, a large timber tract leased to deer hunters. We were going to work early morning firelighting on one of the main roads leading into the Dismal. We chose an intersection on Baker Road, about a quarter of a mile into the Dismal off of Gallberry Road, backed our vehicle down a dead end logging road and covered the vehicle with a parachute. I got the deer decoy ready and set it up on Baker Road about a hundred yards past our setup. We were only set up for about five minutes when we heard a vehicle coming down the road. Tony stayed with the vehicle and I walked out to the dirt road and hid in some bushes. The driver of the truck drove past me about twenty-five yards and stopped dead in his tracks. We knew that he could see the decoy.

He sat there for about a minute, and then we heard the shot. I called for Tony to go stop the vehicle, and I walked down the road to the truck. When I got there, the man said that he thought that it was legal shooting time and asked to see my watch. My watch said it was 0623, and his watch said 0622. The legal shooting time was 0625. When I mentioned that he couldn't see his watch without a flashlight, he said, "Let's see what my truck clock says." It said 0618. He had shot at 0605 by my watch. He quickly turned the key off on the truck where we couldn't see the truck clock. "How much is this going to cost me?" he asked. "Can you help me out in court?" Tony replied, "Yes sir. We'll help you out." The charge was night deer hunting, which included loss of hunting license for two years, minimum $250 fine and the seizure of his rifle. Whether it was returned to the hunter would be up to the discretion of the judge.

That afternoon I met Tony at the patrol station in Washington, and we decided to try the same detail in another part of the Dismal, except this time we would be trying to catch hunters coming out from their deer stands and leaving the area in their trucks. This time we set the deer up on the main road, leaving the timber tract just at the edge of the wood line. Tony let me out and I walked to the intersection of our path and the main road. Tony then quickly backed his patrol vehicle down a dead end dirt path, leaving me at an intersection to work the remote control when it got dark. When it was time, I noticed that I didn't have the remote and called Tony to get him to bring it to me. As I watched him start down the path, I noticed that his vehicle quickly lurched to the left and his headlights started shining in the air. He was stuck. BAD!! We got the decoy up and flagged down a hunter, but he was unable to pull us out. After his last attempt and after he had pulled the steering rod from the vehicle, we decided to call a wrecker. Thirty minutes later, Woolard's Wrecker Service backed down the path, hooked up to us and pulled us from the hole.

September 11, 2001

I really couldn't record these memories without talking some about September 11, 2001 – the day of the attack on the Twin Towers. This day was like none other that I have ever been a part of. I was in the garage that day working on a deer decoy for Gordon Hobbs, Officer 252, in Greene County. I was also having vinyl siding put on my house by Jeff Wade, a local boy from Grifton. Jeff worked by himself and loved to deer hunt, so during breaks he and I would talk about deer hunting. He had come into the garage as I was working on my decoy to watch for a while when my neighbor walked over and asked if I had been watching the TV. I told him "no," and he said that an airplane had just crashed into one of the Twin Towers in New York. He said that he didn't know if it was an accident or not or even if it was a large airplane or a small one. I replied, "You're kidding me! Why in the world would someone be flying so close to the Twin Towers in the first place?" We all went inside the house and turned on the TV to see what was going on.

Almost every station had the exact same picture of one of the Twin Towers burning about ¾ of the way up, somewhere around the 80th floor.

As we were watching the first building burn, another plane struck the second tower and on impact, fire shot out of the other side of the tower. It was very obvious what was going on at that time and that it was no accident. It was unbelievable to see both towers on fire. After a short while, you could see the top of the first tower start to lean a little to the left and then the whole building began to fall straight down as if it had been imploded on purpose. We all sat down in the living room and watched in horror. I had a very sick feeling in my stomach, and at the same time I felt very empty inside. A little while later the second building began to lean at the top, and it also began to fall straight down. It was a sight that I will ever forget. The TV announcer said that it was a terrorist attack and then announced that the Pentagon had also been struck by a large commercial airliner and yet another commercial airliner had crashed in Pennsylvania. We later learned that this aircraft crashed because of the very brave passengers trying to retake control of the plane from the terrorist in control. Passenger Todd Beamer was on his cell phone and was heard saying to other passengers on United Airlines Flight 93 before it crashed, "Are you ready? OK. Let's roll."

America would never be the same from that point on, and it hasn't. All air traffic across the US was grounded. Nothing was being allowed to fly except military jets.

For the first time in my lifetime I could go outside my home and not hear or see an aircraft in the sky. The sky was completely clear. This also included crop dusters, used for dropping pesticides on crops to cause them to defoliate. It was thought that this type of airplane could be used to drop dangerous chemicals on large groups of people as another terrorist attack. One farmer, I believe in Greene County, tried to go up and dust his crops during this ban, was picked up on radar at Pope Air Force Base in Goldsboro and was immediately met with F-18 fighters from the base and escorted back to Goldsboro. What exactly happened next I'm not sure, but I imagine it wasn't pleasant.

On October 31, 2001 we started bombing Afghanistan and the Taliban Regime, and at the same time dropping MRE, military food packets, to Afghanis fleeing their country to Pakistan. We were two weeks into an Anthrax scare, with the dangerous substance coming through the mail to various building in Washington, including the Supreme Court. Airport security quadrupled. People were buying gas masks on Ebay and Army Surplus stores as fast as they could get them. The stock market had fallen, A LOT! On the bright side, the Bible was the fastest selling book immediately after the bombing, and I had never seen so many people flying the American flag. As a matter of fact, I tried to buy a flag right after the bombing of the Twin Towers and I am still waiting to get one. No one has them. As is the American way, some people ordered hundreds of them and jacked the price up to make a quick buck.

Even some of the stores around town jacked their gas prices up to $1.60 a gallon, expecting the price to go sky high but it didn't. Rumors were going around that by the end of the year gas would be $2.50 a gallon, but in fact it dropped to $1.17 a gallon, lower than it had been in a long time.

January 1, 2003

It was the last day of the deer season for us. I had been working with Milton all day, and we were in the Sunnyside area of Pitt County. We decided to check for deer hunting behind the Santree Trailer Park and look for a small white pickup truck. We had gotten reports from the public about a guy in the truck hunting on registered land here, and I had even written him a citation two years earlier for failing to tag his deer. We entered the area behind the trailer park from the west side and started working our way to line of small pine trees, which separated Lynn Raymond Hardee farm from the Perkins farm. As we got closer to this line of trees, we noticed a small green Ranger pickup parked next to a duck swamp and the line for pine trees. We got out of our patrol vehicle and looked through the window and into the truck to see if there was any type of hunting equipment inside to tell us what kind of hunters we were looking for. We noticed a rifle gun and a box of rifle shells. We decided to wait until dark and check the hunter or hunters as they came back to the truck.

After approximately twenty minutes we noticed two men, each wearing hunter orange caps, walking toward the green truck. When they got to the truck, I asked if they had any luck. I also asked why they were coming back to the truck so early. One young boy spoke up and said that they had seen us pull up and they decided to come and ask us if they had done anything wrong. We told them, so far, no, that we had seen their truck and just decided to wait and check them when they got back. Milton checked their license and, finding everything OK, told the boys that we were leaving and that they still had about forty-five minutes to hunt. Sunset was at 1707 and they could hunt until 1737. They thanked us and we left. As we were pulling out, we talked and decided to put out our deer decoy to test their integrity. Milton dropped me out with the deer, and I found a pretty spot near some small pines that would make a great spot to stick the deer. I set the deer up in some sand and checked the motion of the head to make sure that it would be facing down the path and into the direction of the truck as it was leaving the hunting area. Finding everything the way I wanted it, I walked up the path approximately one hundred fifty yards and found a large bush to use as concealment. I laid out my poncho and began my wait.

I hadn't been there more than ten minutes when I noticed the green pickup leave the area in which it was parked and start our way. I waited until the truck was about one hundred fifty yards away from the deer and, using the remote control, turned the deer head to face the truck. The truck came to an abrupt halt and just sat there with its headlights on the deer. After about two LONG minutes, the cab light came on and I noticed that the passenger was opening his door and stepping out of the vehicle. He opened the door fully and propped himself in between the door jam and the cab of the truck. I moved the deer's head slightly annd flipped the deer tail, and a shot rang out. I yelled for the passenger to step out of the truck and put the gun down on the ground, but his ears must have been ringing from the rifle report because both the passenger and the operator acted as if they didn't hear me and drove to the deer. I called Milton and told him that they were coming his way and he should get ready. I also told him what I had seen. In just a short time, I saw the blue light come on and the truck stopped in the path. After about a thirty minute wait, Milton called me and told me that he was coming to pick me up. He told me that he had charged both of the boys with NDH. He also told me that he asked the boys if they knew what time it was and the boy that did the shooting told him that he thought that they were well within the legal shooting time. It was at this time that Milton reminded the two hunters of my conversation to him concerning the legal quitting time for hunting deer that day.

June 1994

One of the benefits of the job was teaching in the Wildlife Recruit School. In order to teach in the school, you had to first attend and pass a Basic Instructor Course, located in Salemburg, NC. It was a pretty intensive school, lasting two weeks, and it was designed to help an instructor effectively write a lesson plan and present that plan to the class. The lesson plan had to be no more than ninety minutes and no less than eighty-five minutes. Time had to be set aside for questions, visual aids and hands-on aids. During the two-week period you would be called on to give an impromptu five-minute speech at any given moment, so you had to be ready for anything. Once we were asked to be ready to talk to the class when we returned from lunch. It could be on any topic we wanted. I was still unsure what to talk on, but when Julian Alman heard the song "My Girl" on the radio he suggested, "Why don't you teach them to shag?" Well that sounded like a plan, so we recorded the song and had it ready for class. When called to give my talk, I started, "Do Da, Lean and Turn, Boogie—what am I talking about?" No one, of course knew, so I said, "Today I am going to teach each one of you to do the North Carolina, South Carolina nine-step competition shag basic step". Everyone liked that idea and some said that they had always wanted to learn to shag. I gave Julian the cue and he started "My Girl" by the Temptations. I started out with the basic step and then dazzled them a bit with the Duke, Do-Da and The Snake — all shag steps. When I finished, we played the song again and I went from student to student to help them out. I don't think anyone got it during that class, but the instructor liked it, and that was all that mattered.

A GAME WARDEN'S ADVENTURE

One other interesting thing that happened during the course involved another officer named Frank Couch. Frank was always playing practical jokes on everyone. He even changed the combination to my briefcase where I had all of my notes for the class and a half-completed lesson plan that I was working on. Because Frank had conveniently forgotten what he had changed the password to, I thought I was going to have to break the locks on my briefcase to get into it. And that was just one of many things he did. Well, we had just gotten out of class and Julian and I decided to go into Roseboro to eat supper. We saw Frank and asked if he would like to go with us. He replied that he couldn't, that he was too shaken up. We asked him what happened and he told us that he was eating at the Corner Restaurant and looked at the table next to him and saw a little boy choking on his food. He said that he got up and ran to the table, picked up the young boy and gave him the Heimlich maneuver. After a couple of thrusts the food was dislodged from the boy's throat. He said he then went back to his seat and continued to eat his food. Frank said, "I felt a small hand on my arm and looked around to see the young boy that I had saved. The boy looked me in the eyes and said. 'Sir, thank you for saving my life.'"

Julian and I looked at each other and then I turned to Frank and said, "We believe you, Frank. That happens to us all the time. Let's go eat." He said that he was going to stay at the dorm, so we left. Since Frank was such a prankster, there was no way we were going to believe him. The next day when the class met, I stood up and told the class what Frank had told me and Julian, that he was just trying to pull mine and Julian's leg, and to just go along with him if it came up in class. About that time, Frank walked in the room and sat down next to Julian and myself. I turned to Frank and said, "You're not going to believe what happened to me and Julian in Roseboro. We had to save three or four people who were choking all around us. We couldn't even eat our food for saving folks." Frank didn't say anything, and the class started. About halfway through the first class, a lady brought a card to the class and it was given to the instructor. The instructor opened the card and it was from the little boy's mother thanking Frank for saving her son's life. The room went completely quiet, and everyone was looking at me. I raised my hand and asked the instructor if I could say a few words. I told the class what had been going on before this incident and then what Frank had told Julian and me as we were going to supper. I then apologized to Frank (and that was tough) and apologized to the class for trying to get them to play with Frank and go along with his story. From that point on, I was a little skittish on playing pranks on Frank. Well, you know what that did. I was an open target for Frank and his practical jokes, and he never let up the remainder of the two weeks. Of course I had to take it. I wasn't going to say a word.

A GAME WARDEN'S ADVENTURE

Two bear taken illegally with the aid of peanut butter and seized during district wide bear detail in Pinetown, NC

District 2 wildlife enforcement officers inspect boats during a spring equipment check to ensure that they are ready for the spring and summer fishing and boating season. From left to right are Lt. Tony Williams, Sgt. Conley Mangum and Master Officer Milton Jones.

Annual equipment inspection at Kinston Regional Jetport Kinston, NC

Boating
Summer 1979

When I started working boating on Lake Gaston and I was riding with a fellow officer, he told me about a boating accident at the Eaton Ferry Bridge. As told by the officer that investigated the accident, a man and his wife had been out on the lake, having a few drinks and watching the sunset from the vantage point of their boat. Enjoying one of Lake Gaston's many spectacular views was a common occurrence. Unfortunately, so was the drinking part. As in most cases involving alcohol and boating, the couple got turned around when it got dark and didn't know which way to go to get back to their home on the water. I was told that the couple saw lights east of their position and, thinking it was their house, headed that way at a rather fast pace. Big mistake. The operator, again, was operating too fast, outrunning his night vision, and he hit the rocks protecting the road. Their boat traveled straight up the rocks and hit the guardrail hard, and throwing the man, who was operating, out of the front of the boat and into the road. I was told that he began hollering for help as he lay in the road. Not wanting her husband to drown, the wife threw her husband a life preserver. Now normally that would be good thinking on her part, except drinking was involved and her mind was very cloudy. Some time later, a vehicle crossed the Lake Gaston Bridge and the operator of the vehicle saw the man in the road with a life preserver, obviously not drowning, and called the Warren County Sheriff's Department to report a boating accident. Wildlife Officers were then notified for the investigation.

Patrolling boating with good friend Anthony Cox on Tranter's Creek

Since my departure from Warren County in August of 1993 for a promotion in Greenville, lights have been placed on the Eaton Ferry Bridge, making it a safer place to enjoy boating and fishing. It's still a beautiful lake with about three hundred miles of shoreline bordering the NC/VA state line and produces nice striped bass and HUGE blue catfish. Boating at night, though, remains, a very dangerous adventure if you don't have the proper boating safety equipment, operate your boat at a high rate of speed, overrun your night vision and throw alcohol in that mix. If you have an accident on the water, especially at night, you can't wait on the sidewalk for an officer or bystander to arrive and help. If you are not wearing a life preserver, you will drown.

July 10, 1985

I had been working on Lake Gaston most of the day and had just gotten to my home in Macon. I ate supper, played with the kids and we all went for a walk on what we called the "Joggin Road" to get some exercise and unwind. It was just about dark when we got back in. I had settled down in my chair for some TV when I got a call from the Warren County Sheriff Department. One of their deputies was patrolling over the Eaton Ferry Bridge and he had noticed a boat on the rocks of the bridge, approximately five hundred yards from Eaton Ferry Marina. When I say on the rocks, I mean on the rocks. The boat was totally out of the water by about six feet. It had hit the rocks at such a high speed that the boat went up the rocks at about a forty-five degree angle, hit the metal guardrail and slide back down with the bow facing slightly to the left. I got dressed and drove to the Eaton Ferry Marina where I met the deputy. He told me what he had seen and told me that the boat was still there, as he had not left the area. I got the deputy to drive me back out to the boat and drop me off. I took my pack with bug spray, a light, snacks and my ticket book. He stopped directly beside the boat, which was partially hidden from the road because of the metal guardrails running the entire length of the bridge on both sides. I told the deputy to head back to the marina and hide his vehicle.

I walked over to the boat to look for signs of drinking, and sure enough the bottom of the boat was littered with beer cans. There was a 35 mm camera on the floor of the boat by the rear passenger's left side and, OH YEAH, a bag of marijuana on the boat dash, directly in front of the operator's seat. I made a sketch of the boat, noted where everything was located, including the throttle position, and left everything where it was, except for the marijuana. I crossed the road, jumped over the guardrail across from the boat and hunkered down for what could be a long wait. There was very little traffic in that area of the county at night, and it was pretty quiet. The lake was still and a quarter moon was out. You could hear the mosquitoes buzzing around you but not wanting to land on you because of the smell of deet. You can hear forever on the lake at night. Bullfrogs were busy with their low croaking and you could hear bait fish in the water splashing, probably trying to get away from whatever was trying to eat them. I would start to doze off, when a car would make its way across the bridge, and I would have to kneel down to hide behind the guardrail until it passed to keep from being seen. This happened a couple of times, but then I noticed a car slowing down to my location.

Just before it would stop, another vehicle would approach from the opposite direction and the suspect vehicle would speed back up again. The suspect vehicle would go across the bridge, turn around and try to make another approach to their boat. This happened an unbelievable three times before the car got a chance to pull over and stop. When it did stop, all four doors flew open and four young men jumped out the car and ran over to the wrecked boat. While they were working, I stepped over the guardrail and slowly walked toward the boat and four young men. They never knew I was there directly behind them, so I walked very slowly to one of the young men, staying directly behind him. They were talking to each other about the beer cans and marijuana bag and working very hard to get everything cleaned up. I noticed that they did not have a flashlight and I, having two, my work light and a spare, offered the spare light to the first gentleman near the operator's seat. He must have thought I was one of his friends because he said, "Thanks", without looking at me and took the light. I can honestly say they were really doing a good job with the beer cans. I just couldn't stand there without complimenting them to that fact. I asked one of them if I could hold a trash bag for him. The boy looked up at me and you could see it in his eyes. HE HAD BEEN CAUGHT.

I called the deputy back to the scene. I asked who the owner was, and then asked to speak to him privately. I asked him what in the world had happened. He said that he and his friends were camping out in Virginia on the lake and while they were asleep, someone had stolen their boat. He said that it was so late and because he had been drinking, he decided to wait until the next morning to report it to the police. He told me that he went back to sleep and sometime later, one of his friends woke him up, telling him that they were coming back from Littleton, approximately fifteen miles from the campsite, and that he had seen a boat on the rocks of the bridge that looked exactly like his boat. He said that he woke everyone else up and they came to look at the boat and sure enough, it was his boat. I asked him if he wanted to file a police report on the stolen boat and he said that he did. I reminded him, just because we ALWAYS do it, that it was against the law to file a false police report and that the penalties could be high, but he was adamant that he wanted to file the report.

I escorted him over to the deputy and told him about this gentleman wanting to file the report but not to let him sign anything until I came back. I left the boat operator with the deputy and began interviewing the other three men, one at the time. All three basically told the same story, but very little of what they told me was what the operator had said. They each, in their own words, said that the four of them had been out on Lake Gaston that evening and had gotten turned around on the lake, essentially getting lost. As has happened before, the operator saw lights and thought them to be lights on a bridge. Actually, at the time this accident occurred, there were no lights on either the rock portion or the bridge span. The lights that the operator actually saw were lights from waterfront homes across the lake. Thinking that he was going to go thru the bridge, the operator had the boat planed off and then suddenly saw the rocks to the bridge. He tried to turn the boat left but it was too late. The boat hit the rocks at a slight angle, traveled up the rocks until the bow of the boat hit the guard rail. The motor choked off because, as we all know, a propeller and lower unit don't do so well on a pile of rocks. When the forward motion of the boat stopped, the boat slid back down the rocks, but not enough to get it back into the water. That was good for them because the boat had enough damage to the hull to sink, had it slid back into the water.

When the boat came to stop, everyone jumped out and ran down the road. One of the boys called a friend of his to come get them. They then decided to let things calm down and leave the area for a while before they started their recovery of the boat and its contents. As I later found out from my interview with the passengers of the boat, they were all drunk and so they went back to the campsite to wait until morning. I thanked each of the boys and walked back to the patrol car. In front of the deputy, I reminded the operator of the penalties of lying. I again asked him if everything that he told me was true and he said that it was. I told him to go ahead and sign the form. I asked the operator about the marijuana, and he said that he didn't know who that belonged to and that it was probably planted on his boat when they were gone. The deputy and I walked the operator back to the deputy's patrol car and had him sit in the front passenger area. I then told him that he probably was not going to like what I was about to tell him. I advised him that he was under arrest for operating a motorboat while under the influence, reckless operator of a motorboat, possession of marijuana and filing a false police report. The operator went to jail, and his friends got a ride back to the campsite.

Another boating casualty on Songbird Creek Bridge

August 1986

Mike Criscoe, who later became North Carolina's first Wildlife K-9 Officer, was stationed in Vance County, and one night he and I were working night boating and fishing near Hibernia State Park. We started out working the campgrounds for bank fishing, moving very slowly in our boat, just after dark, watching for bank fishing from each of the campsites. When it was dark, whoever was fishing could only hear the boat and not see who was in it because of the campfire or Coleman lanterns on the beach. The campfire and lanterns killed the fisherman's night vision, but not ours. Of course we also had night vision (do you mean night vision goggles?). At one particular campsite I saw two men at the shoreline sitting in chairs fishing and a third empty chair with a fishing rod set in the ground in front of the chair. I told Mike to pull the boat to the shoreline and I would check their licenses. As we approached the two men, college-age kids, bowed up their chests and began cussing whoever was in the boat approaching them. We continued our approach and reached the shoreline. I jumped from the boat and the boys started apologizing REAL fast. I told them to calm down, no problem, that I would have probably done the same thing if I were fishing. I asked the two boys for their license and they were produced. I asked about the third rod, and neither of the boys knew anything about it.

Suddenly another young man exited the tent. I asked him for his fishing license, and he said he wasn't fishing.

That translates into, "Oh crap, they got me." I asked who owned the fishing pole in front of the chair, and he stated he didn't know. I asked if the rod was there when they got to the campsite and he said, "Yeah, that's right". I looked at Mike and said, "No problem, it must be abandoned property. Mike, would you reel the line in and put the rod in our boat?" The young man said he was just a little nervous, which is why he didn't tell us that the rod really belonged to a friend of his whom had just left the campsite to return to Raleigh. I said, "That's not a problem. Just tell him to call me and I will check his license and return the rod to him." The young man said, "It's not my rod and I wasn't fishing, but just give me the ticket." I stated, "Sir, that would not be fair to you, and I have never given a person a citation if he was not guilty. Just tell your friend to call me and everything will be okay." The young man looked at his friend and said, "I was fishing and it's my fishing rod. Just write me the ticket." I said, "Now don't you feel better for telling the truth? Since you were truthful to me, I'll make it so you can mail the fine and cost of court to the County Courthouse in Henderson and not come to court." He was very grateful.

After the bank fishermen at Hibernia, Mike and I patrolled out to the middle of Kerr Lake to work non-compliance of boat lights. The night was very dark with no moon, and the lake was very calm. We turned our boat motor off, left the boat lights on and just sat and listened to boats moving off in the distance. After about an hour, we heard a boat leaving Hibernia State

Park, but we could not see any boat lights moving. The boat sound had turned and was traveling toward Satterwhite Point Marina, approximately four miles south of us. We turned off our boat lights and with Mike operating the boat, we started toward the site of the last time we heard the boat.

About five minutes into our run, our boat went over another boat's wake. Mike turned our boat south and we rode from where we felt the left side boat wake to our right, until we felt the right side of the wake on the other side. We did this maneuver, with our boat touching the other boat's wake on both sides, until the sequence of touches was getting shorter, telling us we were getting closer. I pulled out the night vision monocular and could barely see the boat in front of us. We stepped up our chase, now that we had them in sight, until I saw the other boat turn into a cove on the right side of the lake. As we were approaching, we turned our boat lights on and saw people exiting the boat that was now docked. We approached the dock and asked for the operator of the boat. A man stepped forward and said that he knew why we were here. He said that his boat lights went out while visiting friends at Hibernia Campground, but he had to make it home. I stepped into the man's boat and looked at the boat light switches and they were turned off. I flipped the switch up and both bow and stern lights on the boat came on. I hate it when that happens, especially to the tune of a $76 fine and court cost.

A GAME WARDEN'S ADVENTURE

Summer 1987

One of my favorite people with the wildlife department was Dennis Thompson. I first heard of Dennis when he came to work in Area 4, District 3 as my Sergeant, and I met him for the first time at a retirement party for Al Boone from Nash County. Dennis was the kind of guy who knew everything about everything. He was a smart guy and he liked the same type of things that I liked, including AR 15's, assault rifles and just gadgets in general. He liked to invent stuff or improve on things that were already great products. Like me, nothing he bought was good enough; he always tried to improve it. One day I was working boating at Kerr Lake near Nutbush Campground, and Julian was supposed to pick Dennis up by boat and work the lake with him. I called Julian and told him where I was, and he and Dennis started that way by water from Satterwhite Point in Vance County. I saw them coming and saw Julian set his boat down near Nutbush Bridge. I was still a good way from them, running my boat at full throttle, which then was about 50 to 55 miles per hour, and was going to show my new Sergeant just how well I could operate a boat. I could see it all now — he would go back to our area meeting and tell all the other officers how great I was at operating a boat and how proud he was to have an officer like me working for him. Yes sirree, after this meeting, I would be respected and admired.

Anyway, I had my boat on a plane and was heading straight toward them. When I was almost on top of them,

I immediately turned my boat to the left and at the exact right moment, only about twenty-five yards away from Julian and Dennis, pulled the throttle all the way back. I could just imagine my boat setting down and sliding right up next to their boat. I expected to see Dennis and Julian talking about what a good boat operator I was and I guess I halfway expected them to be standing up and clapping, But what I really saw was a large wave of water and spray from my boat heading to my new Sergeant! Time stood still, and I IMMEDIATELY realized that this had not been a good idea. When everything was over, I saw my new Sergeant wet from head to toe. He looked at me and then looked at his clothes, not saying a word. Everything was quiet at that point, except for Julian. "Yeah! See what you've done! You're in trouble now! That's what you get for showing off!!"

I eased my boat up to theirs, looked at Dennis and said, "I swear, I mean I swear that if you will just forget about this, just this one time, I SWEAR it will never happen again". He looked at Julian and told him to take him to the boat ramp. He needed to go home and change clothes. I never heard about that incident again, at least from Dennis. All the times that I worked with Dennis from then on, he never brought it up. It was over with him and I guarantee that it NEVER happened again and he believed me. Dennis was a man of his word, and later on as we talked and became closer, he told me that he knew that officers made mistakes and he would let one of his officers make a mistake once, as long as he learned from it. He would always let a man try something his own way first because more times than not, there was always more than one way to get a job done. If he knew something was not going to work, he would talk to the officer about it and try to get him to see his point and make a good decision. That was always, to me, the mark of a good leader in any area of life —not just a boss.

Of course, it was another story with Julian. For the next few weeks, all I heard was "Yeah, ole Mangum 'bout drowned the new sergeant. Best boat operator I have ever seen ——- for creating tidal waves. That's what you get for showing off. Just had to show him how good you were with a boat," and on and on and on. He just wouldn't quit. The whole District 3 knew about it before I took my boat off the water that day.

Another thing about Dennis was that he loved to talk. One night he and I were working NDH at the Harman House on Bethlehem Road. We were backed up behind an old house and watching a good field that had deer in it. As usual Dennis and I were talking about anything and everything, well it was mostly Dennis, but I was listening. That is, until about 2200 that night. My eyes began to get a little heavy, and I was fighting going to sleep but losing the battle. The last thing I remember was Dennis was talking about gas powered airplanes, and then I was gone. I must have been asleep an hour and when I woke up Dennis was still going, but now he was talking about AR-15's. The first thing I said was, "Yeah I agree, uh huh." He never batted an eye and kept right on talking. I don't think that he even noticed that I was asleep.

Fishing
September, mid-90s

I drove to Aurora, NC and met with one of my officers to work fall fishing on Campbell Creek, located on the Pamlico River in Eastern North Carolina. We loaded our boat with our wildlife gear as well as a cooler with drinks and snacks, not knowing how long we would be on the river working. The boat ramp, Smith Creek Access Area, is located off of Highway 33 east of Aurora and leads to Campbell Creek. We entered the creek and immediately found boats to check. We began working west on the south side of the creek checking boating safety equipment, fishing licenses and a few nice fish. As we continued to work west, we both noticed a small tri-hull aluminum boat with two occupants who were fishing. They were anchored on a small grassy point and seemed to be enjoying themselves. After working about thirty to forty-five minutes, we decided to check our two fishermen.

We pulled our boat up to theirs and immediately notice two older gentlemen, perhaps in their 70s, bantering

A GAME WARDEN'S ADVENTURE

back and forth about something. We introduced ourselves and asked for their safety equipment. I then asked if they had any luck fishing. One man spoke up and said they had caught a few, but not many. The other gentleman said they had done pretty good but everything they caught was fourteen inches, on the nose. I asked how long they had been fishing and was told two or three hours. I asked if they had kept the fish and was told they kept everything fourteen inches and up, because the size limit was 14 inches. I made the statement, "Sir, you do know that fish kept on ice a while will draw up some." One man said to his partner, "I told you so! You just wouldn't listen to me." His partner replied, "Bullshit! Fish don't get shorter on ice," and off they went into an argument with each other. I interrupted them and said, "Before we go much farther with this conversation, let's just measure the fish and see."

The men slid their cooler up to me and opened it up. From where I was sitting, looking at a half dozen or so speckled trout, it didn't look real good for them. I pulled my tape measure from my pocket, took one fish out and laid him on the cooler top. I pressed the top and lower portion of the tail together and pulled my tape from that point to his bottom lip. Thirteen and three-quarter inches. I said, "Let's try another one". Thirteen and a half inches. After measuring all of the fish, one was legal and the rest short. It was at this point one of the guys began yelling at his friend, "I told you. I told you but you just wouldn't listen." "Well I'll be damned!" was all his partner could say.

I said, "Well guys, I guess we have a slight problem. Now I want you to listen carefully. Which one of you caught ALL of the undersize trout?" I guess I knew what was coming next. "I only caught one and he caught the rest. I told him they would draw up." I said "Now guys, listen CAREFULLY to my question. Who caught ALL of the undersized fish?" After a moment of silence one man spoke up, "I did. Just write me the ticket". The other man said that he would pay half of the ticket. My officer issued one citation to this gentleman for undersized fish and let them keep the fish, since they were already dead. As we idled away in our boat, we could hear them yelling at each other, "I told you they would draw up but no-o-o-o, you just wouldn't listen." The other said, "I have been fishing all my life and I never knew that." You could just tell that these two guys were lifelong buddies that loved to pick on each other. Sort of like two guys that I know.

Fishing
August 1996

I called Marshal Myers and asked him if he wanted me to come down on Saturday and help him work some boating in his area and he said, "Yeah, come on down." I met him at his house in Bath, and we put all of our gear in his eighteen-foot Parker center console. He drove us to a private ramp on Pungo Creek that he had permission to use and we put the boat over. It was a routine day, checking boating safety equipment, Jet Ski operation, possible OWI (Operating While Impaired) violations and some fishing. We worked everything from Pungo Creek to Pantego Creek at Belhaven. Marshal decided to patrol under the Highway 99 Bridge in Belhaven and continue working west. There wasn't a lot of activity in Pantego Creek, and Marshal mention that he had received a received a report concerning someone setting flounder nets in inland waters. At one time this was legal, but that rule had been changed and now you could not set a net in inland waters. The nets we would be looking for would have small brown floats holding the nets up but could barely be seen floating on top of the water.

We followed the creek to the left past Five Pines Island and on the next point, Fulford Point, Marshal slowed his boat and saw a brown cork floating near the surface of the water. As we got closer, we could see more corks just under the surface. I got the boat hook and hooked the net, pulling it to us and the boat. Marshal had found a flounder net, and the more we pulled the net, the more flounder we saw in it. Now all we had to do was sit in the area and see who came to the net. As we had the net up to our boat, I told Marshal to hand me a flounder. I lay the flounder down and spread his tail, and taking my knife I cut a small "V" in the center of the tail. I did the same to about six more flounder from one end of the net to the other. Now all we had to do was wait. Marshal started the boat, and we left that immediate area and found a spot to hide our boat in some tall reeds. This spot he chose was in between the net and the only way in and out of the creek. We got a drink and some snacks and sat down on the gunwales, the top edge of the side of the boat, to begin our wait.

As luck would have it, our wait would not be a long one. About forty-five minutes later we noticed an aluminum boat coming into the creek with a young man and girl. They went around the corner from us and out of our sight, but we could still hear their outboard motor running. Soon the motor began to decelerate and then come to a stop in the area where we found the net. We just sat tight in our boat and waited for them to do all the work for us — take the fish out of the net. About forty-five minutes later, we heard the boat motor start up and head out of the creek past our position. Marshal started his boat, and we pulled out of our setup heading straight for the aluminum boat as it came into view. We motioned for the boat to stop and we pulled our boat up next to theirs. On the floor of the boat were about twelve or so really nice flounder. I spoke to the operator and told him what a nice catch he had. We then began checking his boat safety equipment and found everything in order. I asked where he had gotten all of his flounder, and he told me they had caught the flounder outside of the breakwater separating the inland and joint water boundary. Nets could be set in the joint waters but not in the inland waters.

I complimented him on his catch and reached into the boat to pick up a fish. I held him up, fanned the fish tail and there was my "V" notch. I lay that flounder in my boat and reached for another fish. No "V" in that tail so I dropped that fish back into his boat. I reached for another fish and found what I was looking for again, a "V" notch. I then began dropping the marked fish back into the water, as all of the fish were alive, but keeping one fish, if needed, for court. The operator asked what the heck I was doing. I explained that I was returning all fish that I knew to be taken from his illegally set net that was set in inland water. This is the point that every person, no matter what the charge, hangs his head and asks, "How much is this going to cost me?" Marshal told him to follow us back to Belhaven and he would explain everything to him at that time. That young man had just been "game wardened.

A GAME WARDEN'S ADVENTURE

August 1997

It never fails — just when you think you can get a good nap, a call comes in. I had been working the Pamlico River most of the morning and had just gotten home, changed clothes and laid on the couch for what I thought was going to be one of those "slobbering" naps, where you wake up and drool is all over your shirt, but that was not to be. The phone rang, and it was the Raleigh office calling in an "operating while impaired" report from the Tar River. I don't have a boat myself, so I had to go to Anthony Cox's house and get his boat and then drive to Tranter's Creek and put in. I got the boat up on a plane and started out of Tranter's Creek. I was at the mouth of Tranter's Creek, where the creek met the Tar River, when I met a boat coming to me. There were four people in the boat — two kids, a man and a woman. As I got nearer to the boat, the woman stood up and began waving her arms. I slowed the boat and began idling her way. Before I even reached her, she began yelling at me, saying, "Would you please go make those people put their clothes back on?" What? I asked her to repeat what she had just said and she said the same thing again. "Would you please make those people at the sandbar put their clothes on? They are in a yellow and green jet boat." All I could think of at the time was, "yes ma'am," and I headed for the sandbar.

The sandbar is a place in the river about a half a mile west of the Highway 17 Bridge in Washington, and was a favorite spot for boaters to anchor their boats, get out and walk around in about two feet of water. It used to be a favorite family spot where kids could swim near the boat and parents didn't have to worry a lot about them. You could walk from one boat to the next and talk, party and socialize while getting some rays. Lately, though, the sandbar had become a party spot, and there was always a lot of drinking, littering and riding jet skis. We had received multiple reports of people operating boats while impaired and also of jet skis coming in close to the sandbar, turning hard to the side and then spraying the anchored boats that were anchored. Thinking that this was the source of my report, I headed over and began checking boats, looking particularly for that yellow and green jet boat. It wasn't long before I saw the boat I wanted in the middle of a pack of about fifteen boats. I idled my boat over to theirs and began scolding those on the boat and standing in the water next to it about skinny dipping with families around. Everyone there denied that they were doing anything like that.

Two of the people present were in water up to their waist, and I asked those two men to jump up so I could see if they had their shorts on. Both jumped up, laughing, and both did have their shorts on. I told them that if I received another report about them, I would be back and charge all of them with indecent exposure. They said, "no problem," and I started to pull off. As I was leaving, a man in a pontoon boat motioned for me to come over to their boat. I pulled alongside and one of the men told me to act like I was checking their boat, that they had something to tell me. I asked if it was about the skinny dipping and they said yes, but it was a whole lot more than skinny dipping. I asked him to tell me what was going on, and what he said could have come straight out of a men's magazine. Let's just say IT WAS BAD and it involved five people. He also told me that he had pictures to prove it, and he took a roll of film from his camera and gave it to me. I was furious. I went back to the yellow and green boat and began taking names of everyone even near the boat. I verbally blasted the owner of the boat, telling him and his wife that I knew what they had been doing in public and that they would be hearing from me again, REAL SOON! I left that area and I was so mad, I forgot all about my report and went back to the house.

I contacted my supervisors and told them what I had come across. I told them that the man and woman who had reported this to me wanted the offenders prosecuted and that they would be in court to testify. I then went to the District Attorney's office in Washington and presented the evidence to them. They nicknamed this the "naked boater case" and said that they too wanted it prosecuted. I returned home and began calling witnesses that I had talked to on the water, and they told me that there were two pretty prominent people who were participating in this violation and that I needed to be careful. I contacted my office and gave them the names of these people and the agency that they worked for. Because this involved another state agency, my office decided to turn this over to the SBI. I drove to the SBI office in Greenville, gave them my evidence, told them the story and then left. I believe the SBI cut a deal with the boat owner and his wife, telling them that if they would come clean and tell them exactly what happened, maybe a compromise could be worked out with the DA's office. The deal was, the woman would plead guilty to indecent exposure and the man would not be charged. During the investigation the man's employer said that if he were charged and convicted, he would be fired immediately, so this was a pretty good leverage tool. Knowing what went on in full view of several families on the water, I wasn't very happy, but the SBI had done what they could with the case to get a conviction and so it ended as well as could be expected.

Working Fountain boat race on the Pamlico River, Washington, NC

Wildlife "Conservation"

One job of a wildlife officer is to make sure that no wild animal is being held in captivity unless that person has a captivity permit to do so. Some people know this but most do not, and when they see a wild animal, all cute and cuddly, they just have to take it in to be their pet. The problem with this is that most animals living in the wild have not been around domestic animals, and therefore have not built immunities to domestic diseases. When a "pet" wild animal matures and gets to be a pest or worse, it can be dangerous to the "pet" owner. The owners will then turn the wild animal back into the wild, thinking they are doing the right thing, and those diseases can be carried to other wild animals.

During the spring and summer months, when does are giving birth, I start getting a lot of calls concerning fawn deer, thought to be abandoned, on farms or in back yards. The people reporting the "abandoned" fawns often become very emotional and want to make sure the fawn is taken care of, and that is not a bad thing, sometimes. Sometimes, though, the doe is only a short distance from the fawn when the fawn is "rescued." Other times, if the fawn is reported near a road, it is probably the result of the doe being killed by a vehicle, and the fawn really is in need of rescue. I would normally tell the caller to leave the fawn where it was and not to approach it. If it was still there in the morning, then I would come by and pick it up. When fawns are picked up, we make arrangements to have the fawn transferred to what was called in the 1980s the Caswell County Wildlife Depot. Here we would bring orphaned animals, usually very young, to be re-adapted to living in the wild. Some animals are full-grown but have been raised pets. Therefore they are not afraid of humans and need to be re-acclimated to their environment.

There were times when I would pick up a fawn deer from a concerned citizen and then would have to make arrangements to get our wildlife trailer for the transport. This could take a few days, so I would take the fawn deer home and put them into a large fenced in area that I had and wait. My family did enjoy this brief visit from Mother Nature. This gave me an opportunity to educate my family about deer – why there were born with spots, why their hair is hollow (for warmth, of course,) the location of scent glands and why they are used. The visit was never more than about two days but they did get very attached to the deer, including calling several of them the ever-popular deer name "Bucky".

A GAME WARDEN'S ADVENTURE

Abandoned fawn after mother killed by vehicle

In 1980 I was stationed in Area 4 District 3 in Warren County. Our district had a district meeting scheduled, and our whole team decided to follow each other in two patrol vehicles to the meeting. Once the meeting was over, we were returning to Louisburg, up Highway 39 just south of Bunn, when our Sergeant N.G. Crews looked out of his right passenger window and saw a buck deer being held in a chain link fence. Julian was driving, and he was told to turn around and go back to the house. Sure enough, when we pulled into the driveway a six-point buck was in a six-foot chain link fence just looking at us. Sergeant Crews went to the house and talked to the owner. He explained that it was a violation to keep the deer, and the owner gladly said we could take him. Not having a way to transport the deer, Sergeant Crews called the District 3 biologist, who had a trailer for transporting live deer.

The deer was tame enough that you could go into the fenced-in area and pet him and he would follow you around the fence. The trailer and biologist arrived, and a plan was made to open the cage door, let Sergeant Crews, Julian and I go inside and back the cage to the open fence door, raise the trailer door and "shoo" the deer in the trailer. Once inside the cage, any one of us could walk up to the deer and pet it. Sergeant Crews, wearing his new straw hat, decided that he would pet the deer and walk to the front of the deer where, when the time was right, he could reach down and grab the deer's front two legs. He told Julian to pet the deer and walk to the rear of the deer, and on his cue both officers would grab the deer and carry him to the trailer. It really sounded like a good plan until the cue was given. The deer bucked back and started "boxing" Sergeant Crews with his very sharp hooves, and at the same time he was kicking and struggling to get away from Julian, who in charge of handling the rear of the deer. Well these two grown men wrestled this deer all over the pen, getting the deer on his back only once and then he was up again.

While Crews was struggling, his new hat fell off his head and into the mud. Not wanting to be left out of a capture of epic proportions, I lunged for Crews' hat and was yelling for the two of them to pull the deer over to the pen door. I even got my left arm around the deer waist, pushed the deer down while pulling him to the trailer. Once we got the deer to the trailer, I think the deer realized he could get these three grown men off of his back if he just walked into the trailer, which he did. Crews' hat was a little crushed and muddy, with just a dab or two, (no, it was covered) of deer poop on it. I told Crews those stains would wash right out and it would be good as new. After our failed attempts, our biologist said all we had to do was to walk up to one side the deer while still petting it, and use our left arm to slowly go to the deer belly near the hindquarter. At this point you take your right arm and reach under the deer belly and grasp your hands together. Then quickly lift the deer up by his waist, and the weight of the front portion of the deer would hold him down and he could not fight, because his rear legs were pinned against yours. I think Sergeant Crews liked that idea, but he never came back with Julian and me to get another deer from a pen again. I would say that method of carrying a deer worked out great for him.

October 1985

While in Warren County and working with Julian Alman from Vance County, we got a call from our Raleigh dispatcher that a fox was being held as a pet in a wire pen behind a house. Now wildlife officers, especially in "the day," did not carry catch sticks or animal containers with them everywhere they went. This meant that an officer had to think on his feet when coming across a situation like this, which happened many times. Well, Julian and I pulled into the driveway and knocked on the door, and we were met by the owner of the "pet" fox. We asked for a captivity permit, of which there was none, and we explained what had to be done. Surprisingly, the owner was glad we were there to get the fox. We were told it was a little wild and could hurt someone. You think? Anyway, we walked to the pen and studied on it a while. I looked around a small barn and saw a piece of pipe about three feet long and a piece of rope that was about six feet long. My idea was to fold the rope in half and slide it down the pipe until a loop was formed on the other side.

As my partner opened the screen door SLIGHTLY (I did have to yell at him at one point but I said I was sorry later on) I slide the pipe and loop into the cage to try and catch his leg to drag him out. Well obviously, he had never had this done before, because the fox started running around the cage, doing flips and growling at us. By a stroke of luck, I managed to get the loop not around the leg but around his head. This really was not my plan, but I couldn't get it off so I tightened the loop only enough to where the head would not slip out and pulled. When the fox got to the door, I told Julian "I got him, open the door!" which he did. Instead of the fox coming out peacefully and allowing us to place into a cardboard box (that was not my idea,) he braced both front and both back legs on either side of the door, refusing to exit. Not wanting to lose what grip we had, I pulled tighter on the loop, and you would have thought lightning had hit that fox. All four legs went straight out to the side, and I swear I thought I saw his fur standing up. He quit fighting, and I gently placed the fox in the box. That particular move with the loop gave us enough quiet time to close the box and tie the top down with rope we pulled from the pipe. We then transported the fox to the Caswell County Wildlife Depot facility to be looked at by Wildlife Management personnel and released, if possible, back to the wild.

October 1986

I received a call from a friend who worked with the 4-H in Norlina one night while I was sitting at home watching TV. Glenn called to say he needed help, quick! I drove to his home and met him in the living room. His home was an old two-story house, and it had a fireplace with only a round flue where a stand up stove could be hooked to so he could heat the house. I rang the doorbell and heard Glenn yell for me to come in. I saw that he had a round flue plate (the kind that clips over the flue to keep heat from escaping from the house when it was not being used,) pressed against the flue and holding it firmly with one hand. What tha??? Glenn said that he wanted to hook a wood heater to the flue for heat this winter, but when he pulled the flue plate off, the flue was filled with dirt and soot. He said that he got a pail and hand shovel and when he started to clean out the chimney, a furry foot fell through the dirt into the hole he had just dug out. He told me that he had been hearing noises at night on the roof of the house and thought he might have a wolf rat in his chimney.

These rats are larger than the normal mouse and have sometimes, though not very often or when they are alone, attack people. When I was growing up we had a barn with wolf rats, and the only thing I ever saw one attack was the projectile from a 22 short. Anyway I had to see this rat, so Glenn lowered the plate and I shined my flashlight into the dark hole. Sure enough, there was a small furry leg. I told Glenn that the only way I knew to get him out was for me to make a loop with some cord, slide it through a piece of small pipe and slide the noose into the hole. He said, "Do it." I got everything ready, with my noose about three inches across, and told Glenn to raise the plate up slowly and I would slide the pipe and noose from the bottom into the hole. He did as I asked, and we got the noose in position. Shining my flashlight on the animal, I saw its foot step into the center of the noose and I pulled hard and fast, leaving the pipe in the flue after I cinched down on the leg.

Then everything exploded. It sounded like a martial arts fight going on in that flue, and dust was flying past the plate into the living room. I yelled over the noise the animal was making for Glenn to hold on tight, he's trying to get out. I then told Glenn that I was going to pull our critter out and see what we had. I needed him to raise the plate, making a hole only big enough to get

Two Raccoon cubs rescued from chimney in Norlina, NC

the animal out and then cover the flue QUICK, as there might be more than one. On the count of three Glenn slid the plate up, and I yanked my critter out of the flue. When the dust settled we saw a baby raccoon hanging on the end of my loop. We put the raccoon in a small box and went back to the flue to get another one out. This time it was not quite as exciting, but still fun. We retrieved two raccoons out of the flue and the adventure was over, at least my part of it. I boxed up the raccoons to take to a wildlife animal rehabilitator, and Glenn had to dust and vacuum his house.

A GAME WARDEN'S ADVENTURE

September 1988

On this day I received a report of an elderly lady in Warren Plains, about four miles from Warrenton, being attacked by a six-point buck while she was working in her backyard. I was given a contact person and address and knowing that person very well, I drove to her house. She had a love for wildlife that most people in this world will never experience and her heart has always been in the right place for caring for injured or abandoned wildlife, although she knew she could not legally pen up any wildlife without a permit. I met with this lady on my arrival and asked her what had happened. She told me her deer, one she had raised since a fawn, was now a six-point buck and had been named Bucky. The woman that was injured knew Bucky, and Bucky would hang out sometimes in her yard and just eat grass. On this particular day, Bucky was eating pears from this lady's pear tree. The elderly woman yelled at Bucky to get away from her tree. Well I guess Bucky didn't like what he was being told, so he charged the woman. The woman dropped what she was doing (rightfully so at this point) and started running to her home. Bucky caught up with her, butted her in her behind and knocked her on the ground. At this point, Bucky gored the elderly woman in the calf of her right leg.

The woman got up and again ran for the house with Bucky in hot pursuit. The woman made it inside the house, but Bucky was still trying to get to her. The woman told me she had had enough and was going to get her gun and shoot Bucky, but she felt something warm and sticky in her shoes. It was then that she noticed that Bucky had gored her in the calf of her leg and she was bleeding pretty well. She called EMS and was transported to the hospital. Meanwhile Bucky had run off, and that is when I received the call concerning the incident. I told Bucky's owner that we needed to do something with Bucky, meaning I would come get him with a wildlife transport trailer and take him to the Wildlife Refuge in Caswell County, North Carolina. Bucky's "owner" told me that she would get Bucky and have him ready for transport in two days, which gave me time to get the trailer. At the designated time I arrived and saw Bucky with her "owner" and her young daughter. I back up to the deer and opened the back door to the trailer. She tried to lead Bucky into the trailer but he would not go, so she and her daughter got

Wildlife in North Carolina program at Ayden Elementary School

into the trailer, clapped their hands, whistled and the deer entered the trailer. The "owner" and her daughter hugged Bucky and removed a red ribbon with a bell attached from around his neck. It was very emotional for them, and I have to admit a little for me too. I carried Bucky to the Wildlife Refuge and he was released into a fenced area for deer in the hopes that he would re-acclimate itself back to the wild.

May 1991

During the spring of the year the bear sows, after giving birth and weaning their cubs, decide that it is time for the cubs to be on their own. Since bears are territorial, that means the cubs will have to find their own place to forage for food and exist. So needless to say, spring and summer are the months that we get most bear sightings. I received one of these calls one morning near the community of Oine, NC. The report was of a bear walking around this person's home, and she said was not going to take it anymore. I asked her son, with whom I was speaking on the phone, to not let his mother do anything until I got there to talk to her. He told me that he would try. The home was located in the northern part of Warren County, only about 30 minutes from my house, so I quickly headed that way. Because of how much a poached bear (one killed illegally) was worth in gall bladder, paws, claws, skull mounts and capes, the fines for taking one unlawfully were pretty stiff. Plus, the replacement cost of the bear was pretty significant. Upon my arrival I pulled up to an unpainted, weathered house that looked to be 100 years old down a long dirt driveway.

I got out and was met by the son. I asked where his mother was, and he told me she was in the back yard waiting on the bear. I walked around the house and, sure enough, there she was. She was an elderly black lady who looked to be about 100 years old with her gray hair pulled up. She was sitting in an old ladder back chair and rocking it front to back as if it was a rocking chair, but it was not. I walked up to her and introduced myself, but she didn't seem to be impressed and never looked my way. I asked what she was doing, and she said that she was going to shoot her a bear if he'd ever walk out of the woods. The woods she was referring to were approximately seventy-five yards from where she was sitting, and in between her and the woods was her garden. I said, "You know, you really can't do that and I really wish you would change your mind." "We'll see," she replied. I just shook my head, turned around and walked to the son. "Please don't let her shoot my bear." "I do the best I can but she is pretty determined," he replied. "Call me if she does it," I told him. The son just laughed as I walked away.

Duck Hunting

October 1985

There was a really nice duck swamp just north of Warrenton, near the town of Wise, that I not only loved to work, but also loved to hunt. I knew the owner very well, and he was an extremely nice man. He owned a dairy farm, and his pastures bordered the creek leading to Lake Gaston. Beavers, one of my furry nocturnal semiaquatic rodents, had dammed Smith Creek, and this swamp had quickly become not only my favorite spot to duck hunt, but a favorite of other hunters as well. One particular day I had arrived near the swamp from the southern end to listen for duck hunters shooting. I was about a quarter mile away from the swamp, and the noise from the shots would tell me which path the hunters had used to get to the swamp. Right at shooting time, thirty minutes before sunrise, I heard good shooting near the head of the swamp. I worked my way to the swamp carefully, so as to not be seen or heard, and I could see two hunters about fifty yards from me standing in the swamp.

I watched for a while to see if they were shooting "mud ducks." Mud ducks were ducks shot by hunters who really did not know what they were shooting in the air. To them, it was a duck. The hunter would walk to the floating duck and if it was illegal, the hunter would place the barrel of his shotgun on the duck and push it underwater into the mud where it could not be found.

As I watched the hunters, it appeared this was not happening, and I stood up and told the hunters who I was and that I needed for them to walk to the edge of the swamp so I could check their guns for plugs and bag limit. One hunter shouted back that if I wanted to check them, I needed to come to them. I did not have my waders on, so I took off my coat, laid it on the ground and emptied everything from my pockets to lay on my coat. I picked up a long stick and began wading to the hunters in my uniform and boots. I heard one hunter mumble "Oh shit. Here he comes." When I got to the hunters, I was overly nice to them. I checked the license and bag limits and everything was legal. I then asked to check the plugs in their shotguns. I asked for both shotguns and when I had both of them, I turned away and walked back to the shore where my coat was. I told the hunters, as I was leaving, I did not want to risk dropping their guns or shells in the water. When I was back on shore, I checked the plugs and then laid both guns on the ground with their shells beside the guns. I told the hunters to have a good day, and I left to go change my clothes.

January 1986

Working duck hunting was a whole new animal. It could be the most peaceful work you could do or, as most duck hunters preferred, it could be cold, wet and windy. I was used to working duck hunting in Warren County before my move to Greenville. Most of the duck hunting occurred in swamps built up by beavers, and for the most part the water was not that deep, although there were always holes a person could step in and disappear for a few seconds before resurfacing and spitting water everywhere. I have seen that scenario many times over my thirty-year career, to both hunters and wildlife officers. It almost happened to me one morning when two friends of mine and I were duck hunting near Wise. It was my first time duck hunting with these guys, and also my first time in this particular spot. As I remember, it was a long swamp, as most were with the hills in Warren County, and it was only about one hundred fifty yards wide over to a pretty hardwood point that stretched out into the swamp. Not knowing where exactly to set up to hunt, I followed Carl and John to the swamp until we came to a clearing. At that clearing, there were boards reaching from one grassy area to another going out into the swamp.

I followed my two buddies across the boards until we were about a third of the distance across the swamp, straight across from the point I had been eyeing. We waited patiently, and wood ducks and mallards began getting off the water to our right and flying toward Lake

Gaston on our left and north of us. They were just a little out of our range, but Carl and John did manage to kill a few. I, of course was in the rear of the group where my two buddies had strategically placed me and I was beginning to see that if I was going to shoot a duck, that duck was going to have to walk down the same path we came in on, stand on the bank and quack at me a few times. My thought process was that if John and Carl are killing ducks, they are going to have to go get them, which meant the water couldn't be THAT deep. So I made my move. I told Carl and John I was going to walk to that beautiful point I was looking at, shoot a few ducks, as they seemed to be passing right over the point, and when I returned I would retrieve their ducks.

I then walked out to the end of the board, stopped and began determining the direction I was going to take. John said, "Conley, I don't think I would do that if I were you." I said back, "I have been doing this a lot of years and if I stay to the grass edge I should be okay." John repeated, "Well I wouldn't do it." Carl chimed in, "John, just let him go. He is a trained professional and if he thinks he can do, let him go." Of course, I agreed with him, and I stepped off the board and moved to a large grass pile. The first step was OK, but the second step I wish I hadn't made. I was now in a hole with water to the top edge of my chest waders, with NO feet on solid ground or even muddy ground. My gun, stretching from grass mound to grass mound, was the only thing keeping me from going under AND, as luck would have it, the ducks began to fly really good.

A GAME WARDEN'S ADVENTURE

Carl and John were having a great time hunting, and I was trying to get to some sort of solid ground. The kicker to this is that I was only five feet off the end of the board and shotgun hulls were falling all around me. I looked up at Carl, almost straight up, and said "Boys, I could use a little help down here." Carl, with his soft heart and sympathetic side, replied, "The ducks will quit flying in a little while and we'll give you a hand." I struggled for a bit more and finally got my feet on something solid. John reached over and took my shotgun after I jacked three shells into the swamp to empty it. I struggled back to the boards, at the end of the line by the way, and waited for my duck to walk down the bank, stand on the boards and quack. After all, I am/was a trained professional. Trained professional, my butt. I tried to never use that term again.

Swan hunting with friends in northeast North Carolina

A GAME WARDEN'S ADVENTURE

January 1989

Game wardens are known for a lot things, but their strongest suit is their ability to discreetly approach someone without them ever knowing it. That's called sneaking up. Now there is a reason for sneaking up on a person while hunting or fishing, and that reason is safety. Almost everyone a warden approaches is armed with some type of weapon, whether it is a gun in the glove box of a boat or in a tent or any other type of weapon while in the field hunting. If a weapon is not being used for taking game, then hunters and fishermen typically have one for protection against someone wanting to do them harm or to ward off a pack of coyote or wild dogs. Either way, a game warden HAS to treat everyone as if they have a weapon. He normally works alone in secluded areas, and to get the upper hand on a violator, it is best that he not be seen until the area is safe. For instance, one afternoon in the fall of 1985 I was working duck hunting at the head of Hubquarter Creek at Lake Gaston.

I had seen tracks turning onto a muddy woods path off of the main road, and I did not see muddy tracks on the paved road telling me that a truck and come out of the path. I put my truck in four-wheel drive and began following the tracks. The tracks meandered through the woods for about a half a mile and as I neared the end of the path, I saw two pickup trucks parked. I stopped my vehicle about a hundred yards away and continued on foot to the trucks. When I reached the trucks I began looking into the cabs and I could see camo clothing, steel shot and other items telling me the men were duck hunting. I got the license plate numbers and called them in to my dispatcher in Raleigh, and she gave me the names of the owners of the trucks, which I wrote on a notebook I carried. I found a path with fresh foot tracks and followed the path to a marsh. There I could see where the hunters entered the marsh and continued their walk to a point overlooking open water. I kneeled down in the marsh grass until I was certain how many hunters there were and where they were. I then began to make my way to them without being seen. I was within 100 yards of them and about 70 yards back to the wood that I had just exited. I could hear them talking to each other and occasionally shoot at ducks coming into the creek. I remained still and hidden. As the sun began to set, I heard the hunters getting up decoys and then I heard them starting to walk my way. I got as low as I could, covered myself up with marsh grass and let the hunters walk by me.

When the hunters were about thirty steps in front of me, I entered the pathway and began following them back to the trucks. The hunter in the rear was a person that I was familiar with, and I could hear him talking about the last time he hunted this area. I heard him say, "The last time I hunted here I killed fourteen wood ducks and three mallards. Now that was a good hunt." I wrote the duck numbers he just gave on my left hand and continued to follow them. All three hunters were making so much noise — between carrying five gallon buckets, their waders dragging through the marsh grass and the sucking sound of their wader boots in the water — that no one heard me following. As we got closer to the truck I peeled off of the path to the left and got behind some trees, but I could still see the hunters and their trucks. I watched as each hunter unloaded his shotgun and laid it on the truck hood.

When the hunters had their waders around their knees I stepped out of the woods and said, "Hey Mr. Jones (one of the owners of the parked trucks, but I didn't have a clue what he looked like,) had any luck?" One of the hunters (Mr. Jones) said, "We killed two birds between all of us and that's it." I stated, "Okay. While you guys get your waders off, I will be checking the plug in each of the shotguns." "No problem, go ahead." After checking the shotguns, I found they were legal to hunt with, and I began checking the hunting licenses. As I approached the gentleman I knew he said, "Hey Mangum." I returned the pleasantries saying "Hey ————Did you have as good of a day today as you had the last time you hunted this creek? I watched you shoot that hunting trip, and I think I counted you shooting fourteen wood ducks and three mallards. I was at another location and couldn't get to you that day, but figured I would see you here again hunting." "Mangum, I swear I didn't kill fourteen wood ducks; the limit is five and I have never shot over the limit of ducks." I turned to Mr. Jones and said, "Mr. Jones, didn't you hear him say he killed fourteen wood ducks that last time he was here?" "Yes sir I did, and three mallards," he said. "Write him a ticket." "Well, I'm going to let him go this time. Getting caught telling a lie that big is punishment enough. BUT next time I will".

I was promoted to Sergeant on August 1, 1993 and left the northern piedmont area of North Carolina for the coastal area. The men I would be working with were all veteran officers, all with close to ten years or more experience working the harsh Down East conditions. That is, harsh to me. I have never been around so many mosquitoes, and BIG ones, in my career. In North Carolina there were three duck seasons — two short seasons beginning around the first of October, another one in November, and the long season starting in the middle of December. Our big hunts usually occurred at the Pamlico Point Impoundments on Goose Creek Islands near Hoboken and Lowland at the furthest point east on Highway 33 in Pamlico County. The impoundments were constructed and are maintained by the North Carolina Wildlife Resources Commission to promote duck hunting opportunities for sportsman and are controlled by permit hunting on certain days. There are approximately 754 acres of hunting opportunities at Pamlico Point Impoundments alone, and over 9,400 acres covering seven waterfowl impoundments at Goose Creek. That usually meant pretty good hunting for the hunters, depending on weather of course, but a lot of area to cover and a lot of sweat for the officers who were working.

My first fall working the impoundments consisted of a preseason scout of the impoundments to determine if the ducks were there yet and what impoundments were being used by the ducks. This information would help our officer who worked that area set up his detail and decide in which impoundments to place officers. The temperature in Eastern North Carolina can go from sunny skies to hard driving sleet at the flip of a switch. On one of my scouting trips, the officer with whom I was working tied his boat up to a stake driven in the mud on a small creek on the island. We then walked up to the top of the impoundment dikes to look around. It was about 75 degrees and the reeds, black needle rush and wax myrtle bushes we were walking in were about four to six feet tall. As we walked from one impoundment to the other, the mosquitoes were horrible. We sprayed down with 100 percent deet and still had to cup our hand over our faces in order to breathe. This scouting did not produce enough ducks to have officers sit on any of the four impoundments for any extended time waiting for hunters, but we did make plans to work the 0400 walk-in time.

Hunters were always excited about the duck season and would try to enter the impoundments before the 0400 legal time. No hunter could enter the waterfowl impoundment area before 0400 but many tried, and that was the reason we worked it. I would usually drop wildlife officers on the impoundment dikes by boat about 0300, and they would wait. I would take the boat used for the drop off and after leaving the officer, go to one of the many small grassy islands, hide the boat by pulling up in the reeds and then wait for them to call me, usually under a mosquito net sprayed with 100 percent deet. One morning one of my officers, Gordon, was lying in wait on the impoundment when he saw two men dragging a canoe to the entry gate. One man stated, "We can't go past this gate until 0400," and the other gentleman said, "Come on."

As they pulled their canoe to a spot they wanted, it just happened to be EXACTLY where Gordon was waiting. As they got closer to him, Gordon slid into the tall needle rush on the side of the dike. The first man again said, "It's against the law for us to go into the impoundment now. Hell, it's against the law for us to be where we are now." His partner said, "Look man, there are no officers anywhere near here," as he slid the canoe into the impoundment. Once the boat was in the water, the two men started paddling off. Gordon shined his light on the men and whispered, "Game warden. You need to come back to shore." Both men paddled back and had to pull their canoe and gear back to the entrance gate, where both men were cited for going into a waterfowl impoundment before 0400.

October 1993

This would be my first season working duck hunting with my area. Because I had heard so much about Pamlico Point and the great hunting there, that was where we were going to be on opening day. My officer in Aurora had made all the arrangements for boats and where each officer would be when we got there. Because it was still early for the large concentration of ducks to be this far down their migration route and the weather was very mild, we did not see a lot of ducks but I did get my introduction to this type of hunting. We all checked as many duck hunters as we could near the dikes and some hunters in some very shallow waters, but there were still hunters set up inside the impoundments that had not been checked yet. We were just standing there watching the hunters and I told my men, with much wisdom of duck hunting in the impoundments, "Guys, we need to check the remaining hunters in the impoundments."

One of my officers that frequently worked the impoundments asked, "How do you want to go about this?" I said that I would walk along the grass line that I saw in the impoundments and make my way to them. They could do the same with the other hunters. My officers smiled slightly and said, "Go ahead and show us how it's done," and I did. I started wading into the impoundments as I had planned, and very soon figured out what my officer was trying to tell me. Not wanting to show signs of quitting I continued forward, and with every step I sunk a little deeper into the very soft mud bottom, and I use the word "bottom" very loosely. Approximately thirty yards into the impoundment, I had bottomed out. That is, my crotch and butt were sitting on the mud floor, and my feet weren't touching anything solid. I couldn't turn around or go forward, and the water level was about one inch below the top of my chest waders. All of this, and I started hearing cheers from my officers. Things like, "You're almost to him, keep going," and "That a-boy Sarg, not much further," and then the one that really got my attention, "We'll be in the boat waiting for you when you get through checking him."

With no other choice to make, I decided that it was time to turn around, have my waders fill up with water and crawl out of the impoundment on my hands and knees. I actually did get lucky with this one. I turned around back in the direction of the bank and managed to get one leg out of the mud. This allowed me to get my right knee and shin on the mud floor. This helped me to pull the other foot free from the mud, and once on my knees I could slither out of the mud. It took a while to get out but I finally made it out, and even dry. "Good job Sarg. How many ducks did they have?" One more lesson learned. Officers were dropped off on the dikes, and we managed to check the rest of the duck hunters before we left.

January 1995

Now this was a cold winter for me, especially on the coastal marsh areas of Pamlico County. The weather can range from seventy degrees to ten degrees in a matter of days at this time of the year. The Pamlico Point Impoundments are always the go-to place to duck hunt down east on the Inner Banks. This doesn't by any stretch guarantee there will always be ducks there, but it does up your chances. The impoundments consist of four interlocking impoundments meeting at one corner and forming an island. There are water gates and pumps at this intersection, and it is the point where the water levels in each of the impoundments are controlled. Food sources are planted in the impoundments, and the water level is controlled to produce an area beneficial to migratory waterfowl.

For wildlife officers working in the Beaufort and Pamlico County areas, this means monitoring the cold fronts moving in and also checking the impoundments for concentrations of duck on any particular impoundment. Sometimes more ducks will concentrate in impoundment 3 verses impoundments 1 or 4 due to the direction of the winds. Knowing this helps those officers who set up the duck hunting details to check duck hunters by placing the officers in the best areas to see the most activity. During one particular two to three week spell the temperature had dropped to about fifteen degrees, and the wind was blowing hard out of the north across the Pamlico Sound. My officer stationed in Aurora had made his pre-detail scouting trip and determined where he wanted the officers to be.

Adding to his planning was the game lands restriction for entering the game lands before 0400. This regulation gave every hunter the equal opportunity to be at the impoundments and get a decent spot to set up their decoys to hunt. Prior to this regulation, hunters would come to the impoundments the night before their hunt, set their decoys in the spot they wanted and then camp out on the dikes separating the impoundments. This led to arguing and sometimes fighting when hunters would arrive to hunt the next morning. Thus the 0400 game lands restriction.

This particular morning it was cold. Temperatures had been below freezing for about two weeks, and lows were in the single digits at night. There was a hard north wind, and the daytime highs were never over twenty-five degrees. On mornings like this we could not go over to the impoundments by way of the Oyster Creek boat ramp because the water was frozen, and putting our patrol boat over at 0200 would show a broken ice trail to arriving hunters away from the ramp to the impoundments. This could alert arriving hunters that we were already in the impoundments waiting for them. This meant we had to put the boat over at a different ramp making our boat run to the impoundments a lot longer and a LOT colder. As we got closer to the impoundments, my officer in charge of the detail would tell us which officer he was going to drop off first and where to go to be close to the ducks he had seen earlier in the week. My name was called, and I got my gear ready.

At the appointed time, I jumped off the boat onto the bank of the dike and waited for the boat to leave. It was pitch black. I would scan the impoundments with my night vision goggles, as best I could, to see if anyone was moving or if I could hear anyone. Sounded quiet to me at this point. In fact, when the boat was out of hearing range it was dead quiet, almost hurting your ears quiet. I made my way to a small tree growing on the side of the dike on impoundment 4, which also had some tall weeds. I lay my poncho on the frosty ground and began my wait. I did not notice anyone trying to enter my impoundment before 0400. About 0630 the sun began to rise, first turning the sky a bright orange, yellow, and finally blue. The ground was white from frost, and I got under my poncho and lit a can of sterno to heat up the inside. I decided that I could use some coffee and so took my stainless steel cup out to heat up water on my sterno can.

As the water was getting hot, I would lift the poncho up very slowly to see if any hunters were working their way to hunt my impoundment. Not seeing anyone, I would lower the poncho and continue with my coffee. Man it was good. So good, that I figured I should go ahead and make my breakfast, consisting of fried eggs and hash stirred together in another small pot I had. As it was cooking, I would, again, raise the poncho to look for hunters. I did this another two or three times before 1000, and then I got a call for all officers to meet at the pump house where the impoundments met. I was full and warm when I got there and ready to smoke a cigar. Upon arrival, the first thing I heard was, "What in the hell were you doing over there? It looked like the whole Sioux Indian nation sending smoke signals." I guess that was one small thing I overlooked in my planning and, of course, I had to hear about that all day from my officers. Fortunately, we had very few hunters show up to hunt because of the cold weather.

September 2003

At one time North Carolina did not have a separate teal hunting season. Teal, both blue wing and green wing, are very small ducks that usually appear in Eastern North Carolina just prior to a cold front moving in. They are not much bigger than pigeons and fly very fast and erratically, much like a dove. Because they come down before the cold front, the weather that hunters are often hunting in can be hot and VERY buggy. Summer and early fall are not the times to think you can shoot ducks in typical duck hunting gear. Bug repellent and light weight waders are a MUST. When North Carolina got its first teal season, I think in September 2003 or thereabouts, I began receiving phone calls about the Game Land Regulations for Pamlico Point Water Impoundments. I answered their questions and highly emphasized a LOT of bug repellent.

I knew what was coming, and I actually dreaded working the teal season. The weather forecast had called for above average temperatures, in the mid-70s, for the opening day, which meant huge mosquitoes and water moccasins on the impoundment dikes, so we had to be careful. We did have plenty of repellent, and I had a military no-see-um net to cover up with in case I was dropped out to observe hunters. I never went anywhere during the warm months without my net. We started our detail like all the others, getting to Pamlico Point hours before daylight to be in place to listen for early hunting. Not all of Area 2 would be working the impoundments that morning, as some officers had swampy areas in their county to work. There was a large crowd hunting, and most seemed to be younger hunters, that is, college age and a little older. I think the older duck hunters knew what we knew about this place and this time of the year.

As the officer I was working with and I were riding in the boat checking duck blinds outside the impoundments, we noticed an aluminum boat out in open water with no one in it. Thinking the worst, that someone had fallen overboard, and hoping for the best, that someone's boat had drifted away from some hunters, we approached the boat. When we were about twenty to thirty yards away, both my partner and I noticed two sets of hands holding onto the boat gunwales on the opposite side to us, and fingers were all we could see. We pulled up beside the boat, and there were two young men in the water up to their necks holding on to the boat. I said, "Dang boys. Are ya'll alright?" One of the boys spoke up and said, "We're East Carolina University students, and we were told about the Impoundment area and decided to come try our luck at killing some teal. The weather was so nice all we wore were shorts and t-shirts, and after hunting a while we realized we had made a terrible mistake. We did not have any mosquito repellent. They are HORRIBLE. Do you guys have any repellent?"

We started laughing at the boys and told them to get back into the boat and dry off. "We came with plenty of insect repellent." One boy said, "If you let us use some we won't EVER come back here again." We threw them a can, and for a few minutes it was so foggy from spray you couldn't breathe. They each thanked us, started their boat and made a beeline to the boat ramp. My partner and I looked at each other and said, "Why didn't they do that in the first place?" My partner said, "Yeah, there goes our future. Kinda scary."

Duck Hunting

One afternoon in late October I decided to work some duck hunting in plain clothes at the head of Hawtree Creek that fed Lake Gaston, which is located on the NC/VA line in Warren County. The access to the area I wanted to work would be on a dirt path off of Cole Farm Road. I didn't want to get there too early, as then my vehicle would be seen as other duck hunters arrived. I checked the sunrise/sunset chart and determined that the ending time for shooting ducks would be around 1845 in the afternoon. It was against the law to shoot a migratory bird past the hours of sunset. I wanted my arrival time at the creek to be about an hour before sunset. I pulled up to the dirt path off of Cole Farm Road, got out and checked it for fresh tire tracks. Finding none, I drove very slowly across a field and into some woods. There I parked my truck, a 1966 Ford F100 "three on the tree." I put my hip waders on and made my way to the creek, very slowly and quietly. Finding no one in the usual parking spot, I walked out to the edge of the fresh water marsh, being careful to remain hidden from anyone that may be hunting the marsh by boat. Seeing no one on the creek, I started walking through the marsh to a point where I could watch both boats and ducks coming into the creek. All was quiet until about sunset, 1840. I could then hear a boat motor off in the distance and getting louder by the minute. I found place with tall marsh grass and squatted down, hiding myself from the occupants of the boat. I noticed as it got closer that it was an aluminum boat with three occupants, all wearing camo clothing.

The boat pulled up close to the point where I was, and one of the hunters threw eight duck decoys from the boat into the water. The boat then backed up about thirteen yards and anchored. By this time the hunters were five minutes past legal shooting time. Over the next ten to fifteen minutes, all was quiet. Then I heard wood ducks entering the creek from the north. As they came into view, I counted seven wood ducks headed straight for the decoys. As the ducks made their approach, the hunters readied themselves for the shoot. The ducks circled the decoys and began their descent to the water. Just as the ducks' webbed feet touched the water, all three hunters stood up in the boat and fired. Two ducks hit the water and the other five lifted and scrambled to get away from the shooting. One of those ducks shot landed within 20 feet of me.

When the echo of the shotguns ceased I stood up and said to the hunters, "That was some great shooting, guys." The hunters thanked me and then apologized for setting up on me to hunt. I told them not to worry about it, I was just enjoying the view. I told the group

I would get the duck nearest me and bring it to them. I picked up the wood duck and carried it to the boat while another hunter got the second duck and began picking up decoys. As I lay the duck in the boat, I again told the hunters what great shots they were BUT that they really should have gotten there earlier. I then turned the right side of my hunting vest inside out, revealing my NC wildlife officer badge. I said, "Guys, I hate to tell you this but you guys shot twenty-five minutes past the legal shooting time." One guy said, "DAMN IT!" I stated that I need to see their driver's licenses and hunting licenses, and I also needed to check the plugs in their shotguns.

Finding their licenses and guns legal, I pulled out my ticket book and reached for my pen that was supposed to be in my vest pocket. Nothing. A great case and nothing to write with. I then checked the boat registration and compared it to the owner's driver license. Seeing that the addresses were the same, I reached into my handgun extra drop pouch and retrieved a .357 Magnum bullet. I then used the lead from the bullet to scratch the boat number onto my blank ticket. I could use this information to run the registration, get an address and get up with the hunter the next day. I asked the other two guys their names, so that I would recognize them the next day. Then, again with the lead portion of my .357 bullet, I wrote their phone numbers down to reach them at a later date. I told them, "If I can't get up with you two, I am going to arrest the boat owner at his residence and seize his boat and trailer until our court date and then get warrants for your arrest." They both assured me that I would be able to get up with them. I met with all three men the next day at the boat owner's house and issued citations for hunting migratory waterfowl after the legal shooting time expired.

Life is Short

I rode my motorcycle to a store one day after I retired from the NC Wildlife Commission, picked up a few things and walked to the check out. The young man behind the counter said "Man that is one nice bike you have. I have always wanted one and one day I'll get one." I told the young man, "Son, yesterday I was 18 years old and today I am 63 years old. That's how fast time goes by. If you want a bike, bite the bullet and get it while you are young enough to enjoy it."

There are two days that I remember vividly in my career — the first being the day I started work and picking up my equipment at the Raleigh warehouse with Captain Reuben "Crump" Crumpton. After gathering all of my new wildlife-issued equipment, "Crump" took me out to eat at the Golden Corral for lunch. He wanted to know all about me and where I had worked before. I liked that in Crump. He had a caring heart and gentle nature. He then told me about his career as a wildlife officer, one of which he was very proud. The second day I remember was the day my supervisors came to my house to pick up all my used issued gear on my last day as a wildlife officer. They checked each item off on a list of equipment that I had been issued, shook my hand and told me to "take care." As my supervisors pulled away from my house, I remember watching them and thinking "Well, that's it. Twenty-nine years is over. Man, that was fast."

Again, thanks to all the people I have met and became friends with over the years and for letting me into your lives. We shared both good times and bad times together. We also shared some very personal information with each other, just needing another person to talk to. Always remember, what we shared will always be safe with me. That's what friends do.

And now, on to better things.

Worth the wait. Cape Lookout, NC

Made in the USA
Columbia, SC
16 January 2018